CHARTERED
WEALTH SOLUTIONS
Retire Successfully

Message from the Directors and Shareholders of Chartered Wealth Solutions

This book is a culmination of our life experiences and our learnings from our clients on how to retire successfully.

For years we believed giving a detailed financial plan was enough; but we have learnt that each client has a unique story, and individual dreams for their lives in retirement. So, essential for a comprehensive retirement plan is firstly having a life plan, and then a financial plan that enables that life.

Thank you to each and every one of our clients. Live the life you always dreamed of. Enjoy the book, share it with friends, and your sharing will pass on the core message: being prepared for retirement can make it the best years of your life.

Best wishes
Barclay, John, Kim

December 2015

Dear Mrs Perchtold,

This is something I ghost-wrote on behalf of a client last year. It has some great material on all sorts of aspects of life – no matter how far off retirement is! Enjoy.

Giselle

Retiremeant

Kim Potgieter

Stonebridge books

Twisting the Kaleidescope

Do you remember that feeling of joy as you turned the kaleidoscope and the shapes and colours magically shifted, creating a whole new picture?

I am passionate about people living fulfilling and significant lives, especially in retirement. I am also convinced that the right attitude and perspective are essential to achieving this.

When it came to writing this book, I loved the idea of the kaleidoscope as my motif, because just one small shift can change the whole picture. So it is with your perspective on retirement (indeed, on your life!). If you can see retirement as a start rather than an end; as plump with possibilities rather than a narrowing of life; as a chance to make dreams come true rather than relinquishing them, then you can truly have a second half that is better than the first.

This book and my website can encourage you to make that small change in perspective (perhaps for you it might be a big change in perspective). You know what your true feelings about retirement are and, even if they are already positive, here is an opportunity to open your horizons even more.

I would love to hear of your own kaleidoscope shifts. Feel free to email me at kim@retiremeant.co.za.

Happy reading ... and enjoy those shifts in the kaleidescope!

First published by Stonebridge, an imprint of Jacana Media
(Pty) Ltd, in 2015

10 Orange Street
Sunnyside
Auckland Park 2092
South Africa
+2711 628 3200
www.jacana.co.za

ISBN 978-1-920292-32-4

Names have been changed to protect the identity of the individuals.

Cover design by Adrian C Lombard
Set in Sabon 11/17pt
Printed and bound by Creda Communications
Job No. 002388

See a complete list of Jacana titles at www.jacana.co.za

Contents

Acknowledgements ix

Foreword xi

Chapter 1: Knowing Me, Knowing You 1

Chapter 2: The Ten Retiremeant Truths 15

Chapter 3: The Power is in the Planning 33

Chapter 4: Me, Myself and We 45

Chapter 5: Money and Me 59

Chapter 6: From Money to Meaning 75

Chapter 7: The Balancing Act 95

Chapter 8: Bring on the Balance 107

Chapter 9: A Bucket Wheel with Balance 131

Chapter 10: Making your Money Work in Retirement 145

Concluding Thoughts 166

Resources and Recommended Reading 167

Praise for *Retiremeant* and Kim Potgieter

"*Retiremeant* is a must-read for everyone wondering "What's next?" in life. Kim Potgieter, a certified financial planner and lover of life, uses the kaleidoscope as a metaphor for growth and change. Kim provides a holistic approach to financial life planning. In an engaging conversational style, she shares her own and other's stories, offers terrific exercises and tips and invites you to explore what's important to you so you can add the 'A' to your retiremeAnt – enabling your money to help you retire to a life of meaning and fulfilment."

– Dorian Mintzer Ph.D., BCC, Retirement, Money and Relationship Coach and co-author of *The Couple's Retirement Puzzle: 10 Must-Have Conversations for Creating an Amazing New Life Together* (Sourcebooks, 2014)

"Kim's wisdom and professional experience make *Retiremeant: Get the most meaning for your money*, a 'must read'. Both practical and creative, Kim's work challenges you to go beyond what you already know to possibilities that you may never before have imagined. Her kaleidoscope metaphor is perfect for imagining the shifts that could bring to you your plan for a most fulfilling life!"

– Roberta K. Taylor, Retirement Transition Coach and Co-author of *The Couple's Retirement Puzzle: 10 Must-Have Conversations for Creating an Amazing New Life Together*

"I initially resisted attending a financial life planning meeting … I was not convinced that the process would interest me, or that it would be relevant to my life. Having spent some time in just such a meeting with Kim, I see it is about much more than checking a balance sheet. Relating my money to my life and my goals has been a freeing and energising experience, and I feel empowered to be involved in the family's financial planning. I now see the success of my business as a means to buy my villa in Greece, among my many dreams to be fulfilled."

– Miranda Isaakidis, Chartered client and business-owner

Praise for *Retiremeant* and Kim Potgieter

"I have been a financial planner for many years and always prided myself on understanding my clients' needs. It was a unique experience to be on the other side of the process, when Kim helped my wife, Bev, and me, tackle our procrastination regarding a decision to immigrate to Australia, to join our children and grandchildren. Kim, as the only practising qualified financial life planner in South Africa, was not only qualified to help us, but she also has a passion that goes beyond asking the right questions.

"Kim's compassion and insight enabled Bev and me to express how we actually felt: desperate to move, frightened to commit to the reality. I am of the firm belief that Kim's methodology is the only way forward: looking after your wealth and taking your lifestyle into account.

"To fulfil the tapestry of your own personal financial and lifestyle kaleidoscope, this must-read book will challenge you as the patterns of your life change for the better."

– Lionel Karp, Certified Financial Planner

"Everyone over the age of 35 should read this book – it's such a lovely mix of personal heart, expert advice and practical how to! Kim presents a definitive heartfelt guide to making sure that your retirement is both meaningful and rich. This book is shaped around Kim's invaluable contribution to modern wealth retirement – filled with inspiring true client stories, practical insights, 'how-to' advice, and most importantly 'heart'!

"You are in expert hands. Kim has studied with some of the world's leading retirement and financial planning experts, to bring you everything you need to know to plan your retirement successfully. She also adds her wealth of knowledge as a leading, respected, wealth retirement specialist."

– Colleen-Joy Page, PCC ICF certified coach, Managing Director, InnerLifeSkills Coaching International

Acknowledgements

"Families are the compass that guide us. They are the inspiration to reach great heights, and our comfort when we occasionally falter."

AMERICAN POLITICIAN, BRAD HENRY

I count myself very blessed that so many people have played a role in the creation of this book; I am doubly blessed that they are all family.

Thank you, my husband, Gys, my sons, Ryan and Josh, and my daughter, Gabi, for your abundant love and consistent support. To my parents … you have gone but remain in my heart, and I am grateful for your commitment to me as I grew into the woman I am today.

I have always felt the encouragement of my Chartered Wealth family – John and Barclay, you have supported my growth and creativity; I have learnt, with the staff, how to create and deliver excellence – thank you for partnering with me in our journey of exploration.

This book took some time to come to fruition, partly because I doubted that I could be an author; my very special friends encouraged me for three years, reminding me that the book is a voice with a very important message that needs to be shared.

I thank our clients – so many of them will recognise their passions, fears, lessons, evolution in the stories shared in this book. Thank you for your honesty, your warmth, your willingness to share. I look forward to many enriching years to come.

Finally, this book would not have been of publishing quality without Giselle Willcox and Kim Forbes, who crafted in better English the message I felt so comfortable speaking about, but not so confident in putting to paper with the same skill. I am most appreciative, also, of the professionalism of the publishers, Jacana – thank you for being so easy to work with.

Kim

Foreword

"What lies before us and what lies behind us are tiny matters compared to what lies within us."

AMERICAN PHYSICIAN AND POET, OLIVER WENDELL HOLMES

Retirement is a merging point like no other. It is where the horizontal equator of personal means crosses the vertical axis of personal meaning. The difficulty and impact of this crossing are difficult to exaggerate. I view this crossroad as one of three existential transitions in life: the first is graduating from school and wondering what to do; the second is questioning one's career choice in mid-life; and the third is when we come to "graduating" from a career in general – this idea called retirement.

In the traditional retirement discussion, much more consideration has been given to your place on the horizontal line of material means and not nearly enough to the vertical axis of discovering. But that is changing. There are many forms of capital to consider in the retirement equation and only one of them is material in nature. There is your intellectual capital, your experiential capital, your relational capital and your spiritual capital. "How will you invest who you are?" is the most important question you can answer in regards to retirement. I often tell people that the right time to "retire" is on the expiration date of their intellectual and experiential capital. When you no longer desire to keep it current, it's time to move on to the next act.

People struggle with this transition and for good reason. It is an unnatural transition in the course of life. It is not an organic transition like growing up, getting educated, having a family. It is a manmade, institutionalised construct imposed upon our working cultures for the past 130 years and, in my opinion, has run its course. Retirement today at 62 or 65 is nothing more than an artificial finish line that we have every right to run right past or to jog completely around, if we so desire. Those age-markers – invented in times when people retired at 62 and died at 64 – have no significant relevance for the age we live in today.

Today the most pressing question as one approaches the retirement stage of life is not how much life you have left but how much life you have left *in you*. The answer to that question is complex. To answer the question requires a thorough inventory of what is in you. This process may require an MRI of your soul: illuminating your wiring, your experience, your lessons gathered, your aspirations and, ultimately, your purpose for the time ahead. This book, for you, can be that MRI.

There are plenty of thinkers on this planet and there are plenty of doers. I know my fair share of both. I know very few, however, who have successfully amalgamated the two. I know very few people like Kim Potgieter. On second thought, I don't know *anyone* quite like Kim. She's an inimitable persona with an indefatigable level of curiosity regarding what makes life work. Kim is a thinker *and* a doer.

Kim and her business partners came to the US and spent an unforgettable week with me exploring and discussing *Financial Life Planning, The New Retirementality, Return on Life*, and other ideas that have been a big part of my life's work. A year later she arranged for me to come to South Africa to introduce these concepts. In the years since, Kim has continued to study, refine and facilitate money/life discussions and has become possibly the best retirement coach on this planet. I'm continually amazed and thrilled at the work she has been doing.

I've never met anyone who cares as much about the money/life dialogue as Kim does. She has literally travelled the world to glean every bit of insight and wisdom she can gather on the topic. She is relentless in her quest to make the discussion better, more meaningful, more lasting – and more impactful. This book is evidence of her quest. I love Kim's insatiable appetite for what is meaningful. And I love what she is bringing to you, the reader. She's not talking at you, she's living it and sharing it with you.

If you want the optimum life dividend out of your retirement years, I would suggest becoming Kim's client. If that's not possible, then my next best suggestion is to read this book, which you are doing. And I assume that you're reading this book because you know there's a great deal of life left in you.

– Mitch Anthony

What if the second half of your life could be better than the first? And what if this could be achieved simply by changing perspective, by shifting thinking?

CHAPTER 1

Knowing Me, Knowing You

"There is no law of history any more than of a kaleidoscope."

– Victorian essayist, John Ruskin

What if the second half of your life could be better than the first? And what if this could be achieved simply by changing perspective, by shifting thinking?

And what if this book could help you achieve that?

The content of this book is a distillation of the years that I have spent in financial life planning, mostly for those in or approaching retirement. My first-hand experience means that I am witness to clients retiring, often retiring from who they were meant to be and not to who they were destined to become. I have seen people giving up. I have seen many losing themselves in the challenges and transitions that life presents. But I have also seen people grasp hold of the possibility of making life in their second half a life of significance. These are the people who choose not to see retirement as an end, but as a beginning – as a rite of passage in the process of life. These are the individuals who have inspired me.

And so, my greatest hope in writing this book is that you will be inspired, that you too can belong to that second group – that you will make every day count and that you, along with English playwright, Robert Browning, may be able to say: "Grow old along with me! The best is yet to be ..."

You will see that I have chosen the kaleidoscope as a metaphor for growth and change represented in this book. Imagine that you, at this point in your life, picked up a kaleidoscope – that all-too-familiar cylindrical object containing coloured glass and reflecting mirrors – and that you held it up against the light. As you did so, you saw myriad colours and configurations changing before your eyes. By seeing those shifting perspectives, you saw the world in a whole new way. Well, that is exactly what I envision for you and me as we work through this material together. Yes, I would love for this book to read as a conversation between you and me – and for you to believe that you and I are friends. And that together we hold our beliefs and assumptions up to the light for the possibility of a tiny shift in perspective on the world – and on ourselves – as we know it.

Now, you may be thinking that retiring is mostly about money. And there is some truth in that. After all, how can a person retire if they don't have enough money? In addition to that, though, I have learned valuable lessons about retiring and am convinced that retiring is about much more than how much we have – or haven't – saved. Retirement should be about getting the most from your money – and your life. I firmly believe that the insights I have gained, mostly from my clients and their stories (I share many of these stories under the sections marked Face to face), are of value to anyone who is looking for a significant second half. Some insights have come from my own story.

Me

The early deaths of both my mother and my father made me mindful of life and its meaning from a relatively young age. My father was killed at the age of 59 following a hi-jacking and my mother passed away at the age of 64, after a nine-month battle with pancreatic cancer. Both my parents died young. And both of them had put much of their lives on hold. Like many people, they were waiting for a time when they could live out their dreams meaningfully. But for them, that time never came.

As the daughter of a mother and father who were taken too soon, I have come to be determined to live each day to the full and not to put off what I want to do for someday in the future. Seeing my parents lose out on the opportunity to enjoy what they had worked long and hard for made me resolute in my decision to help people reach not only their retirement goals, but also their life goals. As such, I don't want you to put your life on hold "until you retire".

My mom and dad – and my brother Bruce and I – were a middle-class family, financially better off than most South African families. As such, I attended St. Andrew's School for Girls, a prestigious private school in Johannesburg, South Africa and, to a large degree, my family enjoyed the benefits that come with a privileged life. But sometimes privilege comes with a price because, in truth, my family was dysfunctional around money. In my home, money was wrapped up in power, control and a not unhealthy dose of unhappiness. You may have observed other families like this in your own life. Or maybe you recognise your own family.

While the picture to the outside world was of an idyllic life – we seemed to have everything of the very best – the reality was that my mother lived a life of constraint. Normally, mothers get to make decisions around most of the details of their children's lives.

My stay-at-home mom did not even get to decide what to cook for us for dinner each night. That's because my dad kept our meat in a freezer in our garage and would apportion it to us as and when he saw fit. She couldn't even use the telephone when she wanted to! The freezer, the tumble drier and the telephone were all locked away, with my dad the only one with the key – and therefore the control. It was a control over her, over us all. When Christmas time came, he would buy my brother and me extravagant gifts, but sadly, give my mother only a small allocation of funds – and just before the 25th – so that her gifts to us were last-minute and meagre in comparison to his. My clearest memory around money is the image of my mother running out of the house and down the road with me in her arms – all the way to the hospital. I had severely burnt my feet by getting into a bath of near-boiling water. On that day, she had no telephone to call for an ambulance, no car to get me to the hospital (the spare car was locked and my dad had the only key), and no money for when she got there.

It is not how much one makes but to what purpose one spends.

Victorian essayist, John Ruskin

Having said that, my father could be generous with money. My clothing came from exclusive boutiques, with designer jewellery the only fitting accessories. Indeed, he threw lavish seafood parties when he wanted to and the wine bottles from his excessive wine collection were so numerous, the wine expired before it was ever drunk. But his generosity was always on his own terms and there is no doubt that my father derived his sense of security by controlling the money – and the people – in his world. Strangely, or possibly precisely because of this, I spent the early years of my life looking for my father's approval. This is testimony not only to the complexities around family dynamics but the love, which, despite everything, binds us together. Needless to say, though, from this confusing and contradictory context, I have noted two strong attitudes to money within myself: a taste for the finer things in life – which young teenager gets showered with Swarovski crystals? – and a determination never to be dependent on another person for my financial security.

Despite this rather uncertain start, I found I loved everything that had to do with living life. (Can you tell this from my choice of chapter title? Who loves life and does not love Abba? I am crazy about their music.) And food was – and still is – a passion of mine. And so, after a Degree in Industrial Psychology from the then University of Natal, I started a catering business with a friend. More than to food, however, my pull was to people, to engaging with people, working passionately with individuals and putting my organisational mind to work in bettering the lives of those with whom I came into contact.

Then, as many women did at the time, I grabbed my chance at marriage when it came along. I was in pursuit of the perfect, white-picket-fence life – right down to the his-and-hers matching cars and a beautiful bay-window in my suburban home, which was the envy of many of those who visited. This is not to mention the magnificent and towering Christmas tree that touched the roof every year, so grand was it, and – wait for it – two perfect dogs named, yes, Chelsea and Chuckles! The perfect life brought me the perfect son, Ryan (he really *is* perfect) – all at the age of 25. But sometimes, even the most "perfect" lives have to face up to the reality that there is more to perfection than the picture of it. And so, at the age of 28, I got divorced.

Being financially independent was important to me and so I supported myself through my years of singleness, remarrying in

1999. In 2001, my second son, Josh, was born. I sold my catering business to focus my energies on being a stay-at-home mom. If you're a mother who has done the same, you will know that this is not as easy as you would think. Talk about testing your sanity! Thankfully, my husband, Gys, was extremely supportive of my decision – and supportive of our family financially. I loved being a mom, but I was not comfortable feeling financially dependent on someone, and there was a voice inside asking some difficult questions: What is next for *you*, Kim? Where are *you* going?

You've had that voice talk to you too, right? I had a strong sense that there was something else out there to which I could add value. Well, I began to listen to that voice, to learn to become introspective and to look inside myself for some of those answers. As such – and with my background in Industrial Psychology – I registered with UNISA (the University of South Africa) to study Clinical Psychology for three years. Paying attention to that little voice made me sure of a couple of things: I knew I wanted to work with people and I knew that whatever it was that I would end up doing would be in the area of people's relationships with money. But more than that, I had absolutely no idea.

In the midst of this uncertainty, I fell pregnant with a little girl in 2003, the same year that my father was killed. To my mind, my pregnancy with my daughter, Chloe, was a precious and timely gift. I felt it was the universe compensating me for the loss of my father, which had come as a devastating blow to my family. But loss would be mine for longer, as Chloe was born with only half a heart and died after taking just a few first breaths. Have you ever felt that sorrow strikes for longer than it seems possible for a human heart to cope with? Well, if ever I felt it, it was during this time of overwhelming grief.

"Family is not an important thing.
It's everything."
– *Lucky Man: A Memoir*,
Michael J. Fox

These experiences brought me to a personal crossroads. With so much having gone wrong in my life in such a short space of time, it was the perfect moment for me to fall apart. It really was. But was falling apart what I wanted for my life? Was that how I wanted my story to end? Mentally, it was a fight-or-flight moment for me. Was I to accept defeat and retreat into a world of cynicism and heartache? Or would I choose to make something of this pivotal moment? I chose to fight. I made a decision, right there and then, to fight hard to find my life purpose (we all have a core life principle – whatever resonates with us is our purpose) and to explore ways in which I could use these experiences and what I had learnt so far for my life going forward.

So what was the universe trying to tell me? That was what I wanted to find out.

You, me and money

What the universe didn't need to tell me was that I was intrigued by the world of financial planning. I had been reading financial magazines for as long as I could remember – even attending retirement talks and conferences in my twenties. I was always the youngest person there, never actually quite sure why I *was* there! I remember being asked by course delegates why a woman in her twenties would be attending a conference on retirement. My response? "It's never too early to learn." And what I *did* learn was that these conferences on retirement focused wholly on the financial aspect of retirement – how to invest your money, how much money you needed to retire and how to get away with paying the least tax possible. They offered a doom-and-gloom approach to the concept of retirement and offered next to nothing about life. I knew at an intuitive level that retirement was not just about money, that money was only one aspect of it.

In my readings, I had come across an article by Andrew Bradley, the then CEO of financial services group, Acsis. To my mind, Andrew sounded like someone who knew what ethical financial planning was all about. My experience of financial planners up to that time had been of well-gymed salesman-type men who came to your house to persuade you to buy a particular policy, with commission awarded to them! I was impressed by Andrew's article: it was an article on professionalism, on his view that there was a need in the industry for holistic financial advice to be given by degreed, and therefore professional, advisors. This made sense to me, especially for my purposes – of facilitating healthy relationships between people and their money.

So what did I do? I stalked the man. Not really. I just called him. He did not know who I was but was kind enough to take my call. And I, a thirty-something-year-old woman he had never heard of, simply stated that I wanted to play a part in transforming financial planning in South Africa. Andrew certainly was helpful. It was a wonderful life lesson to learn, that sometimes people can be very kind to you. Even if they are strangers.

Andrew's advice to me was that if I wanted a voice in the industry, I needed to get a Postgraduate Diploma in Financial Planning in order to become a Certified Financial Planner (CFP®) and then to contact him again. I had no industry experience so I had to do a lot of convincing of the Head of Financial Planning at the University of the Free State to allow me to enrol. I studied full-time and, with the help of some kind people along the way, passed with three (out of four) distinctions. A year later, I phoned

Andrew Bradley again and announced: "I have my diploma. What now?" He met with me, and referred me to two forward-thinking financial planners he knew: Barclay Hoar and John Campbell. These two men were about to change the course of my life. And they had no idea that I was about to change theirs.

Barclay and John were – and still are – owners of an independent boutique financial planning business, Chartered Wealth Solutions, which truly made its clients the focus of its business. They agreed to hire me as a para-planner. Despite having absolutely no idea what a para-planner was, I accepted! I wanted a foot in the door to an industry that I felt was calling me.

I tried my hand as a para-planner, but soon realised that I was completely unsuited to the position; one requirement was computer proficiency, and I was sadly lacking in these skills (something we neglected to discuss in my interview!).

With my lack of knowledge of, and experience in, the processes of financial planning at the time, being relieved of my para-planning position was a real possibility. Since I also could not fulfil my passion for people in what was largely an administrative role, I resigned from my paid position at Chartered Wealth. I continued, however, to go into the office daily, still unsure where my future lay. All I knew was that it felt right to be there. I just needed to find how I could add value and stay true to myself. I know that not everyone has this luxury but I so strongly believed that I could add something to the world of financial planning. Exactly what it was, though, I wasn't sure. Courses and books along the way served further to hone my thinking in this regard. One such book and course was by George Kinder, author of *Seven Stages of Money Maturity* and a man considered by many to be the father of financial life planning, something different from financial planning. George's philosophy resonated with me. So off I went to the UK to begin my one-year journey in pursuit of my Registered

Life Planner certification from the Kinder Institute.

After John Campbell won Financial Planner of the Year from The Financial Planning Institute, he visited the USA, where he came across a book by Roy Diliberto entitled *The Next Step: A Practical Approach to Merging Your Clients' Money with Their Lives*. This introduced me to the work and ideas of industry-pioneer, Mitch Anthony. Mitch's ideas made sense to me and I believed that they had immense value to add to the world of financial planning.

By now you won't be surprised to hear that, yes, I phoned Mitch Anthony in the USA. And simply asked if I could come and visit him. My partners John and Barclay were suitably impressed with my forthrightness and decided to join me on my pilgrimage to the Land of Plenty. If you're a financial planner who is familiar with the work of Mitch Anthony, you will know that agreeing to random visits by complete strangers is not what he does. Nevertheless, Mitch gave us training in financial life planning. For four full days. In his home!

My time with Mitch, and with other industry experts along the way, has set the tone for much of who I am, what I do and much of what I have learnt. And there is much that has been learnt. Take for example this point: it is not just a client's money that is your client, but the client him- or herself. Yes, it seems like an obvious point to make. And yet there are thousands of financial planners who do not operate according to this principle. How can you invest a client's money if you know nothing about the life that that client wants to live? Our time in the USA was indeed a turning point and further honed our thinking and business strategy. Armed with eight books that Mitch had written and a world of knowledge, John, Barclay and I returned to South Africa ready to re-think financial planning in South Africa.

In the course of this trip, Barclay and John changed their perspective on me and the role I would play at Chartered Wealth.

They had seen my motivation and the initiative I took to go to the USA, and my passion for the way in which life planning could enhance the planning process. I had been bringing new ideas to the company, and my role had become an inspirational and advisory one. They revised their idea of having only two shareholders for the company: Barclay and John were innovative and forward-thinking businessmen and recognised that I brought different dimension to the business, offering something that would add to making our offering distinctive. I negotiated with my husband to return to work, only three days a week … but life planning became my purpose, not my job, and I was soon working full-time at the work that I knew I was meant to do, and became a shareholder of Chartered Wealth.

We decided to focus on the area of retirement. Our thinking was that people who are a little older in life take money matters seriously – sometimes even too seriously, as we came to find out (more on freeing your money up to enable you to live your happiest life later in this book). My own personal losses had made me rethink everything – from what it means to be alive to what it means to really have a life. So much so, that Chartered Wealth Solutions and I developed the www.retiresuccessfully.co.za website, designed to support clients near, at or in retirement. I also came to coin the concept, Retiremeant™, an approach to retirement that imbues this stage of a client's life with meaning and purpose, hence the title of this book.

Our work at Chartered Wealth, which now focused on retirement, started to bring much more fulfilment to our lives, and to our clients' lives too! On the personal side, a few years later, my husband and I were blessed with a beautiful daughter, Gabriela. Professionally, the universe was smiling on us too. We won the Celestis Best Financial Planning Practice in South Africa award. With this accolade, we were encouraged to ensure that our clients were truly receiving the excellent service of which we spoke so confidently. One of the most important inclusions to our process was to introduce a *life*-planning meeting as a pre-cursor to the standard *financial* planning meeting. Bringing the *life* element into our financial planning processes offered each client a bespoke service, a plan tailored to their particular needs. This book has been designed to give you a taste of that part of the process.

You, me and this book

Now since you have this book in your hands, I would imagine that you, like me, are a reader. I like to read and I love to learn. I read to learn. I read to grow. I read to implement new and exciting ideas that I glean from a diverse spectrum of sources. I imagine that you do too.

My hope then is that you see this book as a working document. The book, all about retiring, has been designed to make you think about what retirement means to you – and about ways in which you can inject meaning into how, why and when you retire. It has also been designed to include practical exercises and techniques, which I use when working with my clients. The material we're going to engage with, we're going to engage with together. If you have a pen and a journal nearby – or something to make notes with – maybe keep them handy. When you come across something that resonates with you or even something you disagree with, write it down. Or underline or make a note of it in the book.

So, pick up that proverbial kaleidoscope. Hold it up to the light, look through its cylindrical form and rotate that tube ever so slightly. Let's prepare for some new light, some new colour and some new perspective.

Retirement.
It's not what it used to be.
If that's true, then what is it?
Whatever it is, you'll need to
add your "A".

CHAPTER 2

The Ten Retiremeant Truths

"At the height of laughter, the universe is flung into a kaleidoscope of new possibilities."

– *The Wizard of Us*, Jean Houston

This is not the first book written on retirement. And it won't be the last. But it is a book that offers you an opportunity to see things differently – to be open to learning, to be open to possibilities. And even to laughter.

You and this book

Reading this means you've taken an important step towards choosing what your retirement should look like – and not leaving it to chance.

In Chapter 1, I spoke about this book reading as a conversation between you and me. Make this book yours. After all, this book is about *you*. Albert Einstein said that "paper is to write things down that we need to remember". So, if you need to remember it, write it down; make notes in the margin or underline what resonates with you. You'll find that the act of writing things down commits you to action. In this book, you'll find useful, practical worksheets that tailor-make the experience for you and essentially guide you through the processes of retirement planning.

Retiremeant hasn't been designed to be read in one sitting, although you may be compelled to do that and then come back to the exercises. Either way, feel free to read the book as you need to, completing the worksheets that are relevant to you. Or you may prefer to download the exercises, all of which can be found on www.retiremeant.co.za. They're not like typical homework assignments either, where once you've completed them, you're done. Planning for your life – and for your life in retirement – is an ongoing process. Just as the concept of the kaleidoscope suggests, there'll be movement and change in your life still to come. You are changing as we speak; your life circumstances will change. And your bank balance will too. So, as things change, you may want to go back over those worksheets, exploring different answers to the same questions. Let's start with an exercise right now! Grab your note book and have a go at this one.

RETIREMEANT REFLECTION 1 What is it?

Without thinking too much about anything, take two minutes to jot down as many words as you can that come into your mind when you think of what the word "retirement" means to you. Don't think too much. Just do it now.

....

....

....

....

....

Download a free template of this Retiremeant Reflection by visiting www.retiremeant.co.za

How did that go? Was your concept of retirement clear-cut? Did it have a lot to do with money? As you read on, you'll see that this book is not a how-to-invest book. Remember, we spoke about traditional financial planning in Chapter 1? Of course, I – and the company I work with, Chartered Wealth Solutions – offer financial advice; that's what we are qualified to do. But in *this* book, I'm taking things one step back and sharing our philosophy that underpins an approach to money that enables you to live your best life. The aim of this book is to broaden your definition of retirement, to show you that the concept of retirement has less to do with your money than you think – and *everything* to do with you.

Adding your "A" to retirement

This book supposes that your finances are in relatively good order. You might have the money you need to retire – or are at least planning to have it in the years ahead. What this book will do is guide you in making the money you have in retirement work for you, as well as making sure that your retirement is a meaningful experience. That's why I have called it: *Retiremeant: Get more Meaning from your Money.*

I believe – and have seen it come to pass for many of my clients – that you can retire with meaning *and* money.

Do you know that you have a relationship with money? Whether you recognise it or not, you do. I, first-hand, have experienced people's emotional connections with money – and how those connections play themselves out. Your relationship with money influences the decisions you make, how you behave and – ultimately – when and how you retire! This book is your own journey into helping you discover your own beliefs and feelings about money and exploring how those beliefs and feelings may be holding you back from retiring – not just with money, but with meaning.

"Retirement" has become redundant

Retirement has changed. It is only in the last hundred years that the concept of retirement as we know it has even existed. There have been entire books written on the subject but suffice to say the concept did not exist in pre-industrial times. Before Industrialisation, society's older members were not marginalised. Instead, they were given prominent place in their communities for the insight and knowledge that their many years of experience gave them.

Today, everything is different. Mortality rates are lower and life expectancy is higher – thanks to health initiatives, medical advancements, improved education and higher standards of living. The bottom line? People live longer than we expected them to a century ago, with some studies showing that the average person can now expect to live 30 or more years in retirement – a lot longer than initially anticipated. So, chances are that you have many years of life ahead of you. No doubt, your retirement years will represent a substantial slice of time; yet the traditional model of retirement is still touted in our society as if nothing has changed. What does this mean for our concept of retirement? Well, it means that we need a new understanding of retirement altogether. In short, the idea of retirement needs to retire.

After spending many years studying the subject of retirement – along with everything that retirement *isn't* – I have come to a few conclusions of my own. I call them my Ten Retiremeant Truths.

The Ten Retire**meant** Truths

The Ten Retiremeant Truths are the truths or beliefs that I feel we need to embrace in order to be properly equipped for our later years. This is that time in your life for which experts have a host of names: the "third age", the "third act" or the "second half". Author Peter Drucker calls it "Life 2", going on to make the point that while we're over-prepared for our earlier years ("Life 1"), we're entirely *under-prepared* for our later years. Whatever term you choose to use – in this book, I'll be using the terms "new season" and "second half" – any of them is better than the term "over the hill", right? Being under-prepared for our new season is certainly *not* what we want to be.

Let's turn now to some of the findings I have made over the years.

TRUTH 1: It's not about your age

Like almost everything in life, things are not what they used to be. The same can be said for getting old! As you've just read, old is simply not what it used to be: 60 is the new 40. Simply put, we are just living a lot longer – over 100 in many cases.

Where did we get the idea that only the young had anything of substance to offer? Have you ever heard of a 20-year-old prime minister? Or an astronaut who has just turned 18? What is the average age of the American president when he takes office? Nothing less than 55 years. How old are the world's richest people according to Forbes? Their ages, in order from most wealthy are: 74, 58, 77, 83, 69, 78, 73, 85, 91 and 64. That is not exactly young. The reality is that in many fields – education, medicine, business and politics – you may be doing some of your best work and some of your most profound thinking during your second half of life. When it comes to intellectual capital, 65 is our very prime!

> *Wrinkles should merely indicate where the smiles have been.*
>
> AMERICAN AUTHOR, MARK TWAIN

TRUTH 2: Think outside the box

If you choose still to work in retirement – or find that you have to – you won't be satisfied with a repetition of what you have done in the first half. Finding significance in how you spend your time will be a priority; I have learnt this from my clients. This means that we absolutely have to be creative in designing a new career or rethinking our existing one – and being purposeful in what we do, whether it's actual "work" or not. So, let's join forces to think outside the box in the course of this book!

By the time we've worked through this material together, I want you to have a sense that your creativity and set of talents provide the best backdrop to a beautiful picture – a picture of life as you envision it, of the work you want to tap into. We HAVE to find creative ways of attacking this thing called life. Besides, why would you want to just "retire" like everyone else? This is the time when you get to explore life as you never have, to be open to new ideas – a new career even. To transition from a head to a heart connection about the life that you lead and the lives that you impact. Our world is short on role models, on real people who have accomplished great things and who are ready to inspire others. You could see this season of your life as a time of modelling the very best of who you are to pass on to the people around you.

"Life is either a daring adventure or nothing at all."

American author and political activist, Helen Keller

TRUTH 3: It's about more than money

If you want your retirement years to be enriching – and not just rich – it is useful to embrace the view that retiring is not only about money. Having enough money is essential in this life phase, but it's just one aspect to retirement. Retiring is not an *economic* event. It is a *life* event. And as such, it takes into account everything that your life is about.

This means that all aspects of your life come into play at this turning point: money, work, play, relationships, health, learning, purpose and giving back. Your life consists of many facets and some may be more important to you than others. But if you neglect one area, there will be an impact on the others. Focusing solely on your money is short-sighted because your financial plan and the plans you have for your future are intertwined. This means that the way you structure your investments will depend on what you want to do going forward. You therefore need to define what is important to you at this vital stage of your life – and then make sure that you align your financial plan with those priorities.

Have you realised that with your particular talents and unique set of skills, you can add real value to the lives of others in your retirement years? Have you considered the possibility that working does not have to mean that you get paid? It does not mean that everything you do, you have to do for free. We can develop a more holistic approach that integrates your personal aspirations, life stage, family responsibilities, health issues and concerns around money. In the wheel of life, money is just one of the spokes. Yes, it is a necessary spoke. But ask anyone who has a lot of money: it is certainly no guarantee of happiness or personal fulfilment.

"What we have done for ourselves alone dies with us; what we have done for others and the world remains and is immortal."

AMERICAN ATTORNEY AND WRITER, ALBERT PIKE

Often the only observation we've made about retirement is how we *don't* want to retire, as others have. Watching others can be a good starting point for our own journey. They serve as lessons – even as lessons in what *not* to do.

TRUTH 4: Be master of your money

If you had to be honest with yourself, how would you answer the following question: are you a slave to money? Or is money something that you have mastery over?

During our pre-retirement years, our focus is on saving for retirement. Then, when it comes time to retire, we have to shift gear. Now we need to *spend* the money we've spent years saving for, in order to live. For financial guru Warren Buffet the meaning of money has everything to do with allowing him to do what he wants to do – every day.

Ask yourself what the money you have saved is for.

You may have heard of Return on Investment, but have you considered a Return on *Life*? According to *The New Retirementality* author, Mitch Anthony, financial success should be defined as a Return on Life. He expresses this by asking the question: how well are you doing at living the life you want with the money you have? We need to see money as a means for helping us navigate where we want to go. Money should not be controlling us. We should be controlling it. Money should be an enabler: in its right place, money enables you to live life right.

TRUTH 5: Retire with meaning

How often do we look back with regret on an opportunity we never took? Or a chance at something that slipped us by?

Have a conversation with yourself on how to make this season the most meaningful stage of life yet. Have you ever had these thoughts: "I wish I had not worked so hard." What about: "I wish I had had more courage to express my feelings." Or even: "I wish I'd stayed in touch with my friends" or "I wish I'd let myself be happier." And how about: "I wish I'd had the courage to live a life true to myself and not the life others expected of me!" Having a heart-to-heart with yourself will help you avoid having regrets going forward.

Simply keeping yourself out of mischief is not going to be enough to get you through your retirement years! Being busy will help you pass the time but will bring you absolutely no meaning at all, no sense of significance whatsoever. Doing nothing will literally do nothing for you. Plus, there is only so much golf one man can play. Only so many lunches with girlfriends a woman can stomach.

In fact, not only will the idle passing of time feel like a waste of that time, it could even have adverse effects, according to experts. In his article, "Retirement Kills", Stephen J. Dubner quotes University of Zurich economist, Josef Zweimuller. According to Zweimuller's findings, "[A]mong blue-collar workers, we see that workers who retire earlier have a higher mortality rate and these effects are pretty large." The study shows that for every year of early retirement, two months of life expectancy per worker were lost. In short, retirement can be bad for your health. There is even a relationship between early retirement and, yes, death!

TRUTH 6: Retire *to* and not *from*

The concept of retiring "to" and not "from" is really key to my Ten Retiremeant Truths – and it's a principle that plays itself out not only in the retirement space but also in other areas of life.

Have you ever had friends emigrate from the country you live in – just to get away from the issues that caused them worry there? Chances are that they are not completely fulfilled where they are – no matter where it is. The excitement of being drawn *to* something is generally a greater motivator than running away *from* something.

"If one does not know to which port one is sailing, no wind is favourable."

ROMAN STATESMAN AND PHILOSOPHER, LUCIUS ANNAEUS SENECA

Never let the "push" factor of retirement (you might be "having" to retire, which makes you feel "pushed" – or even "pushed out") overtake what should be a personal goal – finding your very own "pull" factor. If you don't have a "pull" factor yet, don't worry. We'll spend some time looking at that. The trick is getting to know yourself and allowing yourself to go on a personal journey to tap into the things that motivate you and make you happy. Once you have a sense of that, you will have a better sense of what will make your future meaningful – and of the things you'd like to retire *to* and not just a job or career you're retiring *from*.

As you reach the artificial finish line approaching retirement, you might be of the belief that you have to stop working. This is not true. We really don't have to. In fact, research shows that people who work after retiring enjoy a better life. According to a study published in the *Journal of Occupational Health Psychology* in 2009, retirees who transition from full-time work into temporary or part-time jobs experience fewer major diseases and are able to function better on a day-to-day basis than people who stop work altogether.

Work does not have to be how you have always done it before. You can restructure your hours, take a pay cut to work in a less stressful position – or even choose to not work for money. The goal here should be to fit work into life, rather than continuing to squeeze life into work. Work can be defined as meaningful and productive engagement for which we receive a financial or emotional pay cheque – or both.

Whether you are being paid or not, you need to feel that you are useful and relevant. Don't limit yourself to what you can achieve in this next life stage. Having a sense of purpose – and adventure – is everything. You can make your retirement the grandest of all life's adventures. Retirement is full of opportunity. It's a chance to reinvent yourself. I encourage you to dream more – and dream big.

> *"Whatever you can do, or dream you can, begin it. Boldness has genius, power and magic in it."*
>
> German writer and statesman, Johann Wolfgang von Goethe

TRUTH 7: You are your greatest asset

You – as in the body you inhabit – are your greatest asset, the means by which you get through this life. Preserving and enhancing this asset is a priority. This means that you need to take your health seriously.

Not unlike a car, your body is the literal vehicle for taking you on the journey that is your life. So, just like a car, the vehicle of your body needs to be looked after and attended to – with the necessary maintenance you need along the way. Just like a car, you need regular tune-ups and oil changes.

So here comes the question: what kind of equipment is getting you along the road of life? Is it a classic performance car or a dilapidated one with rusty brakes? The car analogy is a fun one – and a useful one. In reality, though, a car can be replaced – or essential parts sourced and utilised. Apart from a few aesthetic changes to our human bodies, we can't generally replace the "engines" of who we are. And you will need the use of your body for many more years to come. So, if your body isn't in good condition now, your only option is to restore it.

A classic car that has been restored needs to be running as well as it can. So it is for your body. Even if you have a disability or a physical ailment, you can still aim to make yourself as physically strong as possible – and emotionally also; holistic health means having a healthy mind *and* body. If you listen closely, your body will tell you exactly what it needs. Preserve it so it can take you where you want to go in the years to come.

TRUTH 8: Attitude is everything

Ever hired someone for a position and been inundated with so many CVs that each one sounds just like the one before? What made you choose one candidate over another? Chances are that attitude – a person's outlook, viewpoint, stance, perspective on life – came into play. Something stood out for you; that something was probably attitude. The way human beings choose to respond to life around them is not just anything. It is *everything*. Attitude impacts on how we see life and how others see us.

I believe in this truth so much that I would go so far as to say that if you change your attitude, you will change your retirement – for better or for worse. As Winston Churchill stated: "Attitude is a little thing that makes a big difference." Did you know that a study at the Ohio Longitudinal Study of Aging and Retirement showed that older people with a more positive attitude towards old age lived seven-and-a-half years longer than their negative counterparts? That's right. You can literally live longer by simply changing your attitude.

If attitude is everything, then taking ownership of your attitude is everything too, right? We don't get to choose how long our lives will be. But we do get to choose how much "life" those years will give us. You probably know the famous words of Austrian psychiatrist, Victor Frankl, who was confined to the constraints of a Nazi concentration camp for many years: everything in life can be taken away from you except for one thing, the freedom you have to choose how you can respond to any given situation. It may not seem like much. But Frankl's view is that it is, in fact, everything.

And transitioning into retirement is not just any type of transition. It is a scenario fraught with uncertainty. Letting go of the past, managing your expectations and fears about the future, developing a new sense of self in your later years – none of these is easy to do! But the transition can be a successful one, and it will be heavily influenced by your attitude. Do you see yourself as a victim of circumstance? Or are you proactive about taking charge of the areas of your life that can be improved? Choose to become a positive person. Positive people are proactive people. They aren't defined by external forces. They actively participate in creating the future that they want for themselves.

Your attitude not only affects your perception of retirement, but your approach to the planning process. It will shape what you create for yourself and what you allow yourself to believe is possible. Your attitude is the sum total of your inner positive and negative feelings about yourself, your life and circumstances. Your attitude will be the thing that projects an energy that draws people to you or repels them from you. Attitude is powerful.

This is what Jane Fonda, famous actress and author of *Prime Time,* has to say on the matter: "Almost all the people I have met who are in their nineties or older seem to have one thing in common: positivity. Scientists at the Stanford Center on Longevity adopted the word 'positivity' to express what they, too, have observed. Positivity is an attitude, a way to approach life; it is expressed through humor, gratitude, forgiveness, playfulness, creativeness and adaptability … We can attain these positive attributes even if we didn't start off with them!"

TRUTH 9: If you plan, you prosper

The general rule of life is that if we don't plan, we lessen our chances of prospering. That is not to say that when we plan, we get to guarantee every – or even any – outcomes in life. We might invest in the stock market. Do we have absolute control over how those markets will perform? No. We might buy a property. But can we be sure that the property market will appreciate in line with our expectations? No. And yet, failing to plan ensures that we have absolutely no control over anything. Nothing at all!

So, planning gives us some degree of control of the outcome – even if it's not the amount of control we'd like. Thoroughly planning your retirement takes the element of the unknown out of the equation and puts you firmly back in the driving seat.

"Success depends upon previous preparation, and without such preparation there is sure to be failure."

CHINESE PHILOSOPHER AND TEACHER, CONFUCIUS

This means you have to plan. You just *have* to. Your life in retirement can be what you want it to be – and more. The secret is planning. If you plan, you prosper.

I encourage my clients to think of a puzzle box. The idea may work for you. There are many ways of building a puzzle: some people start with the edges first, finding the corners and all the puzzle pieces with a straight side. Others find a section that interests them – the detail of a building or the intricacies of a tree. Surely, though, everyone building a puzzle needs the picture – on the box itself – as a starting-point, before they get to think outside of it. What is your picture? What puzzle you are building? What does the picture of your life look like in retirement?

So, plan the picture of the life you want before you piece the pieces together. It's the right place to start.

TRUTH 10: Lighten up and laugh

If you are anything like me, you take your life seriously, especially when it comes to the big questions and concerns around retirement. Yet it is also important to find the time and balance to take yourself a little less seriously. Make sure you infuse joy into your world. If we focus too much on our responsibilities, we forget to have fun.

The seriousness of life and all the responsibility that life has brought through the years often weighs heavily on you. It is time to make space in your life for the present and let go of what is no longer serving you. Make space for some fun. Having fun is the most natural human experience and you are always more fulfilled when you pursue enjoyment in your life.

When you play, you feel a childlike freedom and joy that ignites your enthusiasm for life. And learning takes place when you are truly enjoying yourself. It is never too late to engage in activities that bring you happiness; it can be found in a hobby, in travel. Whatever the case, it's important that you pursue your passion and enjoy your life in retirement. Do not forget to laugh. It is the cheapest and easiest mood booster.

> *"To be 70 years young is sometimes far more cheerful and hopeful than to be 40 years old."*
>
> American professor, author and poet,
> Oliver Wendell Holmes Jr

RETIREMEANT REFLECTION 2 What do you want it to be?

Now that you have read my Ten Retiremeant Truths, it's your turn to write. If your retirement turned out to be everything you wished for, what would it look like? Take a few minutes to paint a picture with words about how things would look – and feel! No two person's ideal retirements look the same. There are no right answers here, only truthful ones.

....

....

....

....

....

Download a free template of this Retiremeant Reflection by visiting www.retiremeant.co.za

How have you enjoyed touching on some of the thinking around retirement? Take a moment to reflect on your initial responses to the first exercise. Have your responses changed? Even just a little? If you are feeling a little bit unsure of yourself – or what you think your answers should look like – don't worry. You're not alone. That is why you have this book in your hands.

We are beginning our journey as the kaleidoscope colours are starting to change. I hope you will like the colours you will start to see. They will speak of possibility, hope and the vibrancy of life ahead.

Our dreams can come
true if we have the courage to
follow them.
And what better way
to dream than the Disney way?

CHAPTER 3

The Power is in the Planning

"I only hope we never lose sight of one thing ... that it was all started by a mouse ... more colours blending into a kaleidoscope of Disney characters as a chorus thundered."

AMERICAN BUSINESS MAGNATE AND ANIMATOR, WALT DISNEY

Truth 9 of my Ten Retiremeant Truths says: "If you plan, you prosper." Sadly, most people put more planning into their annual two-week holiday to the coast or their dream skiing trip than they'll ever put into planning for their life in retirement. "That's unfair," I'm sure you're thinking. "There is a *lot* I have planned for in my life – not just holidays! My tertiary education, for example. And what about my choice of career? My car purchases? And the time I bought my house?" Yes, you planned for those. And you needed to. "And that's not to mention my financial affairs," you continue. "My financial planner and I have committed to a financial plan that will ensure I have enough money to retire!"

Please let me stress it one more time. A financial plan is *not* a financial life plan! In my work as a Certified Financial Planner, I have helped hundreds of clients plan their retirement and it has become very clear to me that while there is no denying that money is the key element in any retirement plan, money is not enough to ensure a happy and fulfilled life. Money is a means to having the life you want in retirement. But it is up to you to envisage – and then execute – what you want your life in retirement to look like. So, whether you're planning for that dream cruise or your retirement ahead, essentially, you need to plan. You will enjoy so much more success if you plan.

"By failing to prepare,
you are preparing to fail."

POLITICIAN AND AUTHOR, BENJAMIN FRANKLIN

Okay, so let's get the process started.

See the next few chapters as your own life-planning meeting, designed specifically for the purposes of helping you envision what you want your retirement to look like. It's a process that begins literally with *you* – where you've come from and how you got there – by looking at your money history and principles, and winds its way through what you're going through in this transitional phase.

The "what" and the "how" are key concepts in your journey: not only will you explore *what* you want to be and do but *how* you will do so. This "how" has everything to do with balance. Your balance is, in effect, your integrity and your integrity is of utmost importance. That's why much of this book focuses on the idea of balance – from assessing how balanced you feel your life is to bringing an enhanced sense of balance into your world. Together we will create a bucket wheel which will become the foundation of your financial plan. Here is a diagram that represents the journey you're about to embark on.

FINANCIAL LIFE PLANNING

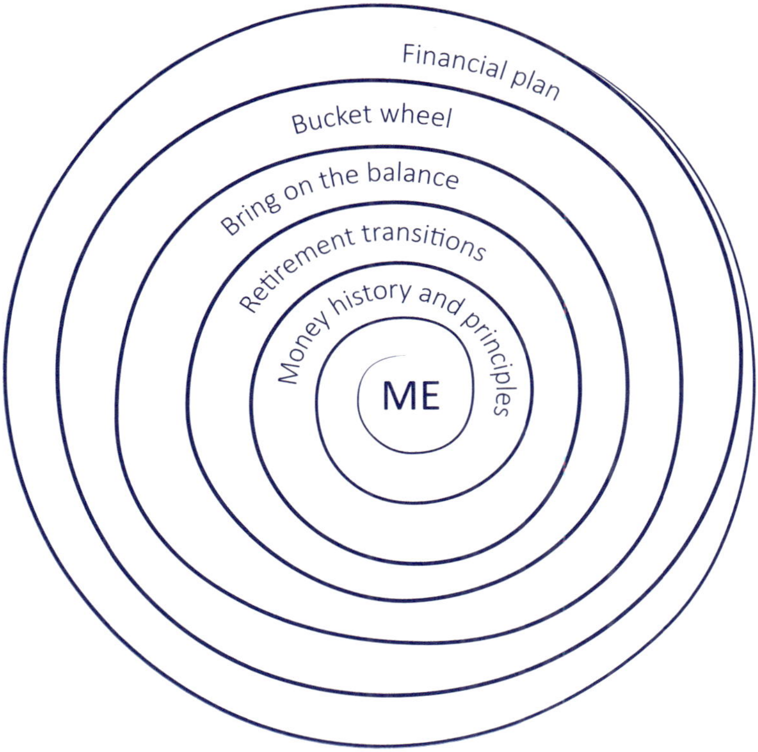

Once we have worked through this process together, you can take this life plan to your financial planner with this particular picture in mind. Your financial planner can best decide with you how to invest your money. The sum of the two parts (your life plan plus your financial plan) is what we at Chartered Wealth refer to as a financial life plan. The clients who consult with me for the purposes of wise investing are first taken through a series of meetings, some content of which is reflected in this book. This is for the purpose of discovering what they want their lives to look like. Only after that, do we look specifically at the money that they have available for investing. My time with clients over the years has shown that people have been so busy working at *life* that they have forgotten what makes them feel *alive*.

What better way to allow this process to get underway than by dreaming – the Disney way?

The Disney way to dream

Some years ago, I attended Disney Institute's Leader Excellence Course and I hold fast to what is now considered a Disney motto: "All our dreams can come true, if we have the courage to pursue them." Just as Walt Disney did, we can let the magic of our lives unfold along this personal journey that we call life. We leave our personal critics out of the room at this stage. Give yourself permission to dream – and to dream big!

From Disney to destiny

Walt Disney built his empire using management strategies now taught in business schools throughout the world. I believe that if we apply Walt Disney's core philosophies, we are well positioned to identify and verbalise our dreams and desires.

I like to take my clients through four thinking processes espoused in "The Disney Way": vision, planning, critic and, finally, action. The life-planning meeting I have with my clients encompasses the dreaming and visioning part of the process. An often-quoted saying goes something like this: imagination is the soil that brings dreams to life. And this is where we get to dig our feet in deep and imagine. And we imagine big!

Sacred to the Disney paradigm is that the voice of the visionary doesn't meet the voice of the critic – not until after the dreaming is finished. After all, are we not our own worst enemies? How often do we tell ourselves that we can't do something? I know I do. As you work through this chapter, make a decision today to leave your critic out of the picture.

Be assured: before any action plans are agreed on or financial steps taken, the critic is allowed back into the process. The critic is key to the integrity of "The Disney Way", key to the entire journey you make. In this chapter, we hone in on vision and planning. The critic and action steps are taken into consideration in the last chapter of this book as you finalise the steps you will take to retiring with more certainty.

So, if I were taking you through the process face-to-face as you explore options around your retirement, this is where we might start.

On the following page is the Retiremeant Reflection 3 exercise to do.

RETIREMEANT REFLECTION 3 How big can you dream?

This exercise is all about dreaming. We are not letting the critic into the room at this point but taking this moment to envision.

Step 1: Vision

Take a moment to think of a dream you have – a big one – for your retirement. Maybe a desire you've always had? Something tucked away at the back of your mind? This is the kind of something that, if there was nothing standing in your way, you would see as the fulfilment of your life's ambition. Yes, there may be the voice of your inner critic at work right now. Take a breath. Acknowledge your inner critic's voice. And somewhere in your thinking, reassure this voice that it will be heard in time. But this particular moment is for letting your imagination run wild. Visualise your dream coming true. What dreams do you still want to achieve?

....

....

....

....

....

And more specifically, what would your retirement look like if it turned out well?

....

....

....

....

....

Step 2: Planning

Believing that there is every possibility of this crazy, beautiful dream coming true, you're going to take a few minutes to plan some actual, practical steps towards helping your dream come to fruition. You could mind-map those ideas or write those thoughts down. Even draw pictures if that feels like the appropriate thing to do.
Go slowly; now is not the time to let your inner critic loose. In this moment, give yourself what you need in order to achieve your goal. Identify some milestones along the way to reach in order to achieve your goals.

....

....

....

....

....

Download a free template of this Retiremeant Reflection by visiting www.retiremeant.co.za

Face to face

John and Denise came to see me to invest money that they had inherited when their daughter, Jennifer, aged 30, was killed in a skiing accident. Despite the time that had passed since the event, they were still struggling to invest this money because, to them, it represented their daughter's death and their subsequent grief.

Before we could explore their investment options, I needed to spend time with them discussing how best to approach the money and how to make the money represent something positive and not be a reminder of the loss of their precious daughter. In our time together, we shared experiences; Denise, John and I laughed and cried together and shared memories from our pasts. Together, we decided that it was important that they do something significant with the money – so that their daughter was able to live on in a meaningful way. They needed to create something beautiful out of what had been bitter pain.

During my sessions with them, I drew on some Disney dynamics. We needed to find a way that my clients could envision freely – and without input from their inner critics – as to what could, or "should", be done with the money. So, we started exploring questions like: "If this money were to fulfil a life's dream for your daughter, what might that be?" They shared about how their daughter had had a passion for educating – and how much hard work she herself had put into her own education in order to become an attorney. As we brainstormed together, it became apparent that they could best serve her memory by setting up a bursary fund for someone to pursue the same career she had – and study a law degree. To them, this represented seeing the money being used for something positive, something that would be a fitting tribute to their daughter and her passions.

From the vision stage, we then moved into the practicalities, planning how this transition could happen. We looked at the specifics of how much money they had inherited; we took into account that they were both over 60, so we needed to look at what allocations they had made for their own retirement. Both came from families with a genetic history of longevity. And even though emotionally they felt numb inside, they realised that they could still live for 30–40 years. What would their daughter have wanted for them? Would she have wanted them just to survive from day to day and not to feel alive? When we got into the nitty-gritty of planning and looked at their financial assets, it became apparent that they needed some of the money from their daughter's inheritance to be able to retire with enough money to be able to do things, such as go on holiday.

For the critic stage of the process, we gave attention to what could go wrong. We discussed how their critical voice, which had told them to keep all the money for retirement, was in conflict with their vision of giving back something so that the inherited money could become a positive tool for change. They realised that their vision had to be fulfilled in order for them to start gaining acceptance about receiving the money. The process evoked excitement in them; through envisioning, they felt – for the first time – that a cloud had lifted and there was some light in their lives. The critic felt that they might run out of money, and I tackled this by proposing that they opt not to retire but stay working. This appealed to them. We decided to take half the inheritance amount and invest it in their retirement. The other half would be placed in an investment, with the interest earned paying for a bursary for someone to go to university for as long as the funds permitted.

Denise and John showed what can only be described as bravery in tackling the visualisation process. It was a process that helped them to face – and then deal with – their hurt, while at the same time securing their financial future. In follow-up meetings, they expressed that they felt a new lease on life as they could now focus their energy on finding suitable bursary candidates and, in that way, let their daughter's memory live on.

Most of us understand the necessity of having a financial plan. Without one, it's difficult to prepare and save for the life you want to live. However, a financial plan that doesn't take into account your unique circumstances, life goals and ambitions is doomed to fail. This is because even if it makes you money, your life will lack the meaning for you to enjoy it. It is therefore imperative that you think carefully about what it actually is that you want to achieve in life – and communicate this honestly with your financial planner, who can then draw up the financial plan that will help make your dreams become a reality.

"The secret of success is consistency of purpose."

BRITISH POLITICIAN AND WRITER, BENJAMIN DISRAELI

Know what you want

Now that you have allowed yourself to dream, an idea of what you want your life in retirement to look like is beginning to evolve. Even if the picture isn't clear, you are in the process of planting the seeds and the picture is beginning to get clearer. Be patient. As you do more discovery work over time, it will become clearer.

The biggest obstacle to the creation of a meaningful financial plan is simply that most of us can't identify what it is we want out of life on a deeper level. We live in an increasingly frantic world where we are caught up in the act of surviving on a day-to-day basis. At most, we might plan ahead for our annual Christmas break at the coast. Do we spend time introspectively assessing where we want to be in 10 or 20 years' time? We may have a vague idea of "retiring to the coast" or "travelling the world" but have we actually taken the time and effort to plot out exactly what financial steps and actions need to be taken to make these a reality? And at an even deeper level, have we spent any real time thinking about our values and life goals? Or how these relate to our financial planning?

Face to face

Joanne and Peter were clients I explored the Disney concept with. Peter was a cancer survivor, but after a number of years of being in remission, he discovered that his cancer had returned. The couple had planned to carry on working until Peter turned 65. Now, with another health scare, things felt unpredictable once more. We chatted and shared and did Disney visioning together. What would life look like for them if it turned out well, I asked them. It was obvious from our time together that Joanne and Peter wanted to spend as much time together as possible, nurturing each other and making sure that Peter's cancer disappeared for good. Was this possible with the stress of fighting traffic and the pressure of working nine-hour days?

As we explored together, a picture started evolving – a picture of Joanne and Peter moving to their holiday house at the coast. It was a picture that evoked images of them walking together on the beach, taking the time to eat healthily, having the quiet time to be introspective. As part of our process, the "critic" was then allowed back into the room. We analysed the financial figures and reanalysed them. Peter could resign from his job and grant himself a sabbatical during which to fight the cancer and be with Joanne, the woman he loved. Through proper dreaming and planning, Joanne and Peter had put themselves back in the driver seats of their lives and were fighting for a true Return on Life. The lesson is: know what you want.

The key to a happy retirement is not only to be prepared financially but also to be emotionally equipped. Most of us are preoccupied with the accumulation of money as the most important aspect to retirement. This is where we go wrong. Even if we have R200 million in the bank, it is no guarantee of a happy retirement. Yes, a sizeable nest egg may set you up for some comfortable years.

But true happiness and fulfilment will only come with planning and preparation that are in line with the person you are and the dreams you have for your life. Let's make sure then that you have something to retire to.

To my mind, success is where opportunity meets preparation. With reflection, information, preparation and planning, we are well-positioned to increase our chances of being successful, thereby making our retirement the most meaningful season of all. Planning for what you want is everything. Keep turning that kaleidoscope until the picture emerges that is the one you want, full of colour, light, hope and happiness. If Walt Disney can grow an empire from the idea of one little mouse, nothing is stopping you from getting what you want. And if you're still not clear on what it is that you want – well, it's the perfect time to consider the most important part of this entire process: you!

Relationships are everything.
And what's the most important
relationship you have?
The one with yourself.

CHAPTER 4

Me, Myself and We

"We know what we are, but not what we may be."

English playwright, William Shakespeare

When I see a client for the first time, he or she often appears nervous. There is a lot of fear, insecurity and vulnerability around retirement. The future is looming. Waters are unchartered. If this is how you feel, I'm here to tell you that this experience is normal. And what's even more significant is that those feelings – and everything else about you – will offer an entry point to a literal lifelong journey of learning, a journey not just about money, but about you.

Clients who come to see me about investing their money may have no idea that the journey they will embark on begins with them. That journey is not about how much money they have or how much money they want. It has everything to do with a journey of self-exploration. As you open yourself to shifting the kaleidoscopic colours that are your life, so you will see your future through new eyes. And this will be because you see yourself through new eyes.

ME

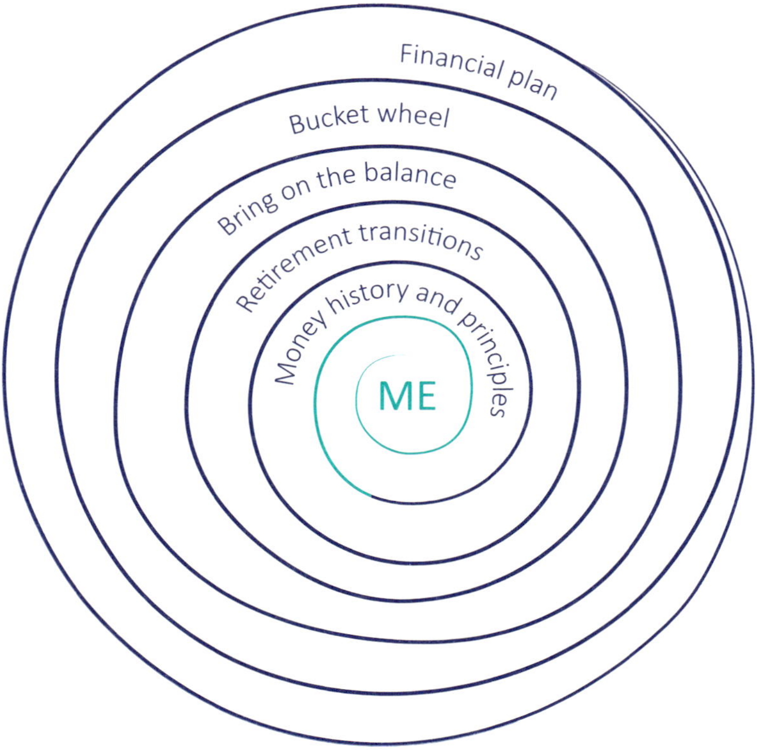

Central to this process is not just you – but you in relation to your significant other. Whether this is a husband, wife, life partner or other family member, I find it useful for financial life planners like me to engage clients as couples. This is because so much of who we are is informed by the relationships we have. Of course, life events such as divorce and death, or a decision to remain single may mean that meetings involve only you. When it comes to the couple dynamic, I encounter some specific scenarios. One such scenario is where men give the impression that they don't want their wives to spend money, the root of this thinking being that they believe their wives spend too much; another that they think they can – and should – control their wives via money. The irony is that once a wife is empowered, she spends less. Research has shown that compared to their male counterparts, women often make wiser stock market investments. Less affected by ego and testosterone, women often operate instinctively, aligning themselves with brands that resonate with them – and to excellent results.

Many of my client couples have never had much-needed conversations about money. Sometimes it is the wife who sabotages the process by not coming to the meetings; sometimes husbands don't want to include their wives in these discussions. As far as I can, I ensure that I engage both parties for these conversations, conversations that will have life-long ramifications. On the male–female front, there are other factors to consider – like the fact that as they age, both women and men change hormonally. Women's testosterone levels increase over time and as such, they gain confidence as time goes on. Might this be evolution preparing women for their predisposition towards living longer? Conversely, men lose some of their sense of confidence and assertiveness as they get older, and this has implications for decision-making and retirement-planning. As you can see, it is useful to have some insight into yourself and your personality as you make significant transitions in your life.

The power of personality

Never underestimate the power of an effective personality-profiling system. Knowing a little more about yourself and what makes you tick will stand you in good stead when it comes to planning for your retirement.

Like it or not, you have as much control over the personality you are born with as you do over the colour of your eyes or the shape of your nose. That is, none at all – well, not without surgical intervention! Your personality DNA is like a psychological blueprint that informs your perception of the world and your basic hopes and fears – right up to how you communicate and respond to others. There is no "right" or "wrong" personality. Your personality is simply the filter through which you experience life. Just because your personality is integral to you, however, does not mean that you can't adjust your behaviour or communication style or response to circumstances around you.

Self-knowledge is the beginning of self-improvement.

Spanish writer, Baltasar Gracian

RETIREMEANT REFLECTION 4 Who are you?

So, are you interested in finding out what personality type you are? If you want to take our particular online personality awareness profile test, visit www.retiremeant.co.za. Once you have done that, I will send you a profile report. This profiling system is one of many you can take and it is one of my preferred methods.

Download a free template of this Retiremeant Reflection by visiting www.retiremeant.co.za

Seeing how your partner may be viewing the same circumstance from a completely different perspective because they have a different personality is enlightening. Add to this the fact that the more authentic you are, the more sincere your interactions with others will be and the more fulfilled your relationships will be. Sharing personality report findings with your spouse can be an eye-opener. I often hear clients say something along the lines of: "Oh, this is why she has driven me crazy all these years!" or "Seeing him in this way makes everything make a bit more sense."

From me to we

Once you have a sense of some of the things that make you tick, it's time to consider the couple connection. Relationships are at the core of our humanity and having a sense of who we are in relation to others is essential to the fundamentals of life – and to the realities of retirement. Whether you are married, co-habiting or dating; whether you're with a husband, a wife, a lover or companion, you're not retiring alone. Even if it is only one of the two of you who is retiring from the formal workplace, retirement is something that will affect both of your lives. When one person in a relationship undergoes a life transition, it inevitably impacts on the other person – and sometimes that impact catches us unawares. As one of my clients once quipped: "I married him for life but not for lunch!" Retirement is a relationship reality. She was not quite prepared for how much time she'd be spending with her better half.

"Everyone is the age of their heart."

GUATEMALAN PROVERB

It goes without saying – although there is much research to support it – that people who have fulfilling relationships with their loved ones live long and happy lives. Sadly, the importance of healthy relationships is often overlooked when preparing for retirement. While there is no denying that planning your finances, health and meaningful activities in retirement is crucial, the state of your relationship is often more so! Yes, it is the difference between a happy and unhappy retirement. It doesn't mean a thing if your bank account is healthy but your heart is in tatters. So why not use this season of life to hone in on the people you love? Retirement is the ideal time to enjoy your relationship with your husband, wife, lover or significant other.

In fact, retirement sometimes prompts you to have to make a conscious effort to interact with others. As you exit a nine-to-five career, you may be hankering after the sense of community that work provided you with. In reality, though, that community probably consisted of work associates you spent a lot of time with, but who, at the end of the day, were merely acquaintances. See this season then as an opportunity to shift gear, to create the space and support for a number of meaningful relationships from various areas of your life – as well as the season in which you have the time to do it! Retirement is a life transition that encompasses not only some changes to your day-to-day activities but some fundamental shifts in the roles and responsibilities that you and your partner have. This is an exciting time. Choose to embrace it!

Do you anticipate facing some relationship challenges as you enter this time of your life? You are not alone and what you're feeling is normal. Each relationship is different and its challenges unique to that particular dynamic but here are a couple of common scenarios I have come across that you might recognise in your own life. How about the situation where the husband has worked outside of the home and the wife has stayed home raising the children? Invariably, she has built up a sizeable social network with her own regular activities and may resent a husband who is now at home during the day, expecting to do everything together. Or what about when both partners are working full time? One partner may be ready for retirement, the other not. Should they both retire together or should they stagger their retirements? Not only will these decisions have a financial impact on their lives, they will also impact on the nature of their relationship.

The third scenario is when one partner is preparing for retirement and slowing down, while the other's career is just taking off. I see this most often with stay-at-home moms whose children have left the nest. Once her children have settled into their studies or their careers, the wife may resume a career of her own by taking a job outside the home – often a job that inspires her and becomes something that she feels passionate about. This can cause a huge amount of relationship tension as the retiring partner, looking forward to spending more time with his spouse, can suddenly feel left out, his picture of retirement slipping away from him. The key to dealing with this, and any, issue is communication!

Face to face

As mentioned earlier, when I run a financial life-planning meeting, I always encourage couples to come along together. As much as retirement is about your individuality, it is also about a shared vision. Moreover, it is not uncommon for communication between couples to be lacking, and having the difficult conversations – conversations about money and the future, for example – is often difficult. Sadly, most couples discover they want very different things and financial life planners, like me, can play an important mediation role.

One particular couple, Moses and Martha, had this very problem. They couldn't see how retirement was going to work for them because they had completely different dreams for their lives in retirement. Martha wanted to travel overseas; she wanted to take dance classes. Moses wanted to stay at home and spend his spare time collecting vintage cars.

After sharing their visions, it became clear to them that they needed two separate accounts of money so that they could enjoy their interests individually. No, this wasn't the conventional retirement that most couples envision, but it worked for them. They both realised that they loved the opportunity to be a little independent – and then felt a renewed connection when they spent time together, each invigorated by the new experiences they were having.

Spending time with your partner is obviously very important, and time apart affords you the opportunity to work on yourself and pursue your own interests. In fact, it's unrealistic to share in each one of your partner's interests. Variety is the spice of life; it's healthy. The key is to listen to your partner and understand what is really important to him or her – and then to be open to the idea of experiencing things apart from each other, as individuals.

Now it's your turn. Let's try our Couple's Quiz exercise to see how ready you are, as a couple, for retirement.

Exercises such as these are great ice breakers into the unchartered and often chilly waters of conversations around retirement. Another exercise that can help you to see life from your partner's perspective is *The Three Chairs* exercise which follows after Retiremeant Reflection 5.

RETIREMEANT REFLECTION 5 Are you talking?

In their book, ***The Couple's Retirement Puzzle***, authors Roberta Taylor and Dorian Mintzer offer a couple's quiz that is a good place to start the discussion with your partner about retirement. This simple questionnaire will help you get a quick glimpse into how each of you views your communication.

Instructions

Put a T after any of the statements below that you believe are true. Notice the areas that you may want to talk more about. Do the quiz separately and then share your results with your partner.

- We have talked about our timetable for retirement.
- We make financial decisions together.
- We know that our roles may change as we go through this transition.
- Having time together and time apart is important to both of us.
- Intimacy and affection are an important part of our relationship.
- We agree on our obligations and responsibilities to family.
- We have planned for future medical and health care needs.
- We talk about lifestyle and where we may want to live.
- Social and community connections are a satisfying part of our lives.
- We have shared values and know what's important to each other.

Scoring

How many Ts do you have in common? Remember this is meant to be a helpful tool for opening up communication. It is not a measure of your relationship.

10: Give each other a big hug. You're in a good place and can be proud of yourself!
7–9: Sounds like you're in sync. Ongoing communication is important as you plan for what's next.
4–6: You're on the right track. Practise listening to each other and sharing what's important to you.
1–3: You're not alone. Many couples need help to be able to talk about important issues related to retirement and what's next.

Download a free template of this Retiremeant Reflection by visiting www.retiremeant.co.za

Two people, three chairs

The Three Chairs exercise or *Wearing Another Man's Shoes* proves powerful in enhancing communication between couples and is an exercise used by coaches all over the world. As the name indicates, the exercise has everything to do with seeing things from a different perspective. By doing the exercise yourself, you will literally put yourself in the other person's position in order to see things from his or her perspective.

The exercise uses three physical objects and requires you to literally move from chair to chair to get that different perspective. Once you've done the practical exercise a couple of times, you'll get the hang of it and will find you no longer need to do the physical exercise itself but can mentally move yourself between the various perspectives.

RETIREMEANT REFLECTION 6 Who is right after all?

Instructions
You will need three chairs about one metre away from each other, set out in a triangle. Think of a situation you have encountered recently with your partner where you each saw the situation from a different perspective. Recall the example and do the following:

First position: Sit in the first chair and relive that experience in your mind from your own perspective. What are you thinking, feeling, hearing and saying to yourself as you look across to the second chair that represents the other person? If you find it easier, write your thoughts down on a piece of paper.

Second position: Now move to the second chair and pretend to be your partner. What is your experience now? What are you thinking and feeling as you look across to the person's perspective as represented by the first chair? Speak out loud as if you really were this person.

Third position: Now move across to the third chair and take a few moments to observe both "people" in the other chairs. Think about how these people have related to each other and to the situation. Take a look at the first chair and ask yourself what advice you could give. In addition to giving you a different perspective, this exercise also has the potential to fix any disagreement you may have with the most positive result possible.

Download a free template of this Retiremeant Reflection by visiting www.retiremeant.co.za

The exercise on the previous page was structured in a way that allowed you to see a situation from three different viewpoints: yours, the other person's perspective and a third position – that of a detached position – that enabled you to see both points of view. It is useful to be able to move from one position to the next as it enables you to resolve a matter with the least amount of conflict. As we grow in ourselves and our relationships, so we mature to a place of objectivity where we can, with distance and clarity, understand the relationships that make up our lives.

Face to face

Ross, aged 58, and his wife, Lisa, came to consult with me not so long ago. Ross wanted to see if they had enough money to retire. He did have a little money to his name but it was barely enough if he wanted to keep up their current standard of living in his retirement. But if Ross stayed in his current job for another two years, he would enhance his retirement savings considerably. The problem was that Ross hated his job and he was adamant that he was going to resign.

I took him through *The Three Chairs* exercise. In the first chair, we looked at his job from his perspective. He was older than his boss and felt constantly belittled by this younger man. He also felt insecure about the rate at which technology was changing and the impact it was having on his job. When he moved into the second chair, we looked at the situation from his boss's perspective. Ross's take on things was that his boss was threatened by him and his constant belittling of him was to make himself feel superior. His boss had told him that he was concerned that Ross was too old and not able to keep up with industry advances and therefore viewed him as "dead weight" in the department.

The third chair helped us to see the situation from a neutral perspective. His concerns were legitimate. But so were those of his boss.

I suggested that in order to deal with his fear of technology, he enrol on a course or two. This would enhance his knowledge base and make him more confident on the technology front. It would also communicate to his boss that he was committed to his career and showing proactivity and enthusiasm by upskilling in a changing environment. Looking at this situation from a different perspective benefitted Ross, Lisa *and* his boss. Ross found new fulfilment in his job with his new knowledge and went on to add value to his company long past retirement age. Lisa felt more secure knowing their investments would have more time to grow.

This preparation time has helped you learn more about yourself and your partner. Years of being together has often taught us how to have an impact on each other and we learn where each other's vulnerable points are: it is important for us to respect these in each other.

There have been a number of situations in which I have seen the value of a husband creating a "man cave" for himself – this is a place in the home (perhaps a repurposed playroom or teenagers' TV room) where he can go to be quiet, where he can spend time in self-reflection, or just pursue his hobby for hours without interruption.

Having the vital open conversation with each other regarding how we see retirement if it turns out well for both of us is essential. Many activities will be shared, while many we will embark on separately, but these open conversations enable us to get each other's buy-in. Encouragement is most helpful as we go through a transition. If you have adult children, having these conversations with them so they feel part of the journey is very useful.

"When we least expect it, life sets us a challenge to test our courage and willingness to change; at such a moment, there is no point in pretending that nothing has happened or in saying that we are not yet ready. The challenge will not wait. Life does not look back. A week is more than enough time for us to decide whether or not to accept our destiny."

The Devil and Miss Prym, Paulo Coelho

So, as the kaleidoscopic patterns and colours of your life shift you into new positions, choose to be open to doing the personal work required to learn more about yourself – as well as more about the people in your world.

How important is your first
money memory?
It impacts how you see money
– and yourself.
Even to this day.

CHAPTER 5

Money and Me

"Forrest Gump had it wrong. Life is not a box of chocolates; it's a kaleidoscope. In the flip of a wrist, realities are shredded and the world takes on a totally new shape."

Them Bones, Carolyn Haines

If author Carolyn Haines is correct and life isn't anything like a box of chocolates – but instead a dynamic process of movement and shift and change – then the changes that come with retirement are not to be taken lightly. Meeting with a financial planner about your money and your future can be a very stressful experience. Whether you've saved well or spent too much, a face-to-face encounter about your future can leave your soul feeling exposed. Even as a CFP® professional, my own planning and processes leave me feeling vulnerable. I find myself making excuses for how I have managed my money – why I have saved what I have and what I need my money to still provide me with. How much more vulnerable is it then to sit and share details of your financial life with a stranger? Even if you have your spouse or partner beside you, the sense of angst does not necessarily lift. Sometimes things feel even worse, especially if – and this happens in many situations – this is the first time that a couple is sharing exactly what their financial positions look like to each other. So, be mindful of this if you meet with a planner. You may find yourself feeling very displaced. It is normal.

One of the questions I ask my clients is this: "What is the money for?" I have learnt that understanding what you want to do with your money is the best starting point for any planner who is going to be managing it for you. Money, after all, is an enabler. It is a doorway that can open you up – or close you down – to your life. Like it or not, money is an essential element of your world. So, with that in mind, how would you describe your relationship with money? Is it harmonious? Complex? How do you see your money? What is it that you want your money to provide you with?

The power of the past

In order to look at your future, it makes sense to dabble a little in the past. I would want to understand as much about you as I could to truly add value to your journey. Before I could offer you insights into where you might be going to, I would want to get some sense of where you have come from – your background, how you went about gathering the wealth you have.

Underpinning an effective financial life plan is your life, as you have gathered by now. As a financial life planner, my top considerations are where you have come from (your history) and how you have got here (your principles) in order to properly understand how you see money.

MONEY HISTORY AND PRINCIPLES

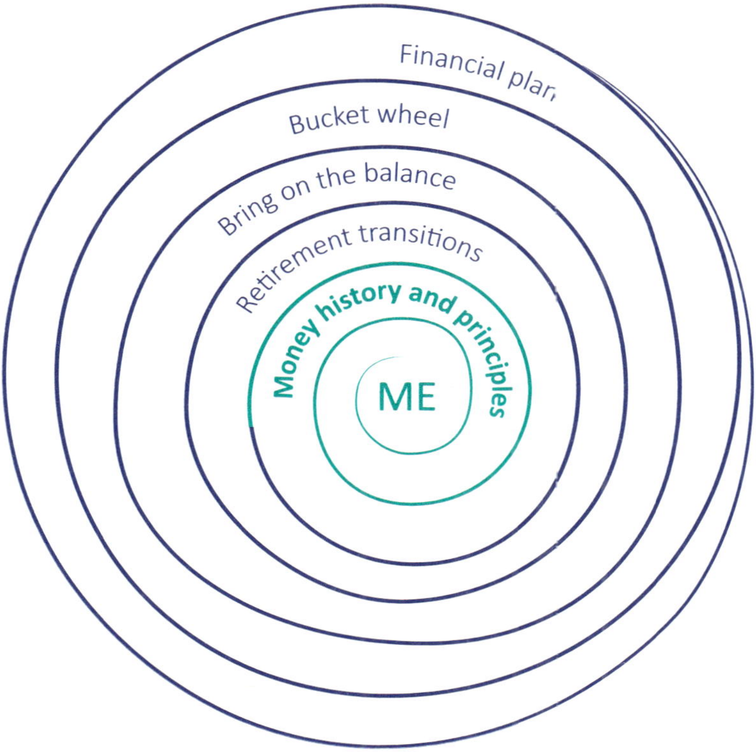

Your financial plan should be designed around what you value most in your life. This means that top of mind is to define what is important to you – and then to align your financial plan with those dreams and goals.

"You are today where your thoughts have brought you; you will be tomorrow where your thoughts take you."

ENGLISH PHILOSOPHER AND AUTHOR, JAMES ALLEN

If you want your life plan to be meaningful, your life itself needs to be meaningful: your life needs to be aligned with your principles. Your principles are indicators of your personal True North, your own internal compass, which plays a role in determining the direction your life takes, revealing the deeper meaning of your life and its purpose. Maybe you have a clear sense of what those principles are. Or maybe your journey is just beginning. Either way, it's important to spend some time, as we will now do, looking at your *history* and the *principles* you live by. Your history is all about where you have come from. Your principles are the things that you stand for and what you regard as important. Together, your history and your principles determine how you think, feel and behave.

RETIREMEANT REFLECTION 7 What do you remember about money?

These questions are for you and your partner to answer around your history with money.

1. What lessons about money did you learn while growing up?

....

....

....

....

....

2. What is your first memory around money?

....

....

....

....

....

3. Who are the people in your life who are affected by the financial decisions you make?

....

....

....

....

....

4. What past experiences with planners stand out in your mind and how have these experiences impacted how you engage with planners now?

....

....

....

....

....

Download a free template of this Retiremeant Reflection by visiting www.retiremeant.co.za

Answering these questions enables you to start thinking more deeply about issues around money and what money means to you – and about whether your relationship with money is based on a belief in your past or a construct of where your life is now and, if your relationship with money is based on something you believed long ago, what that belief is. Communicating these answers with your partner will help you understand your – and your partner's – relationship with money. Let's spend some time unpacking your responses. We'll tackle the first question by looking specifically at one of my client interactions.

Face to face

A couple came to see me after having been married for a number of years and I posed some questions. Of Bill and Sue, I asked: "What lessons about money did you learn while growing up?" Bill's answer? His dad had always communicated the common saying, "A fool and his money are easily parted." His wife, Sue, had grown up in a home where this philosophy prevailed: "If you get money in one hand, don't hold it with the other hand". In other words, her worldview dictated that money should flow out as easily as it flowed in. The messages that Sue and Bill had grown up with were in direct contrast to each other! This is an important piece of information for any planner wanting to engage authentically with a client.

So, how did I advise them? Well, in order to accommodate both of their long-held personal truths about money, we all agreed that Bill's money go towards paying for necessities like food and shelter. That way his money was, in his mind, being put to good use and honing in on the basics, accommodating his more conservative approach. Sue's money, on the other hand, was to go towards paying for luxuries for both of them. In that way, Bill was able to enjoy the finer things in life without feeling his principles were being compromised and Sue could exercise some of the freedom she had grown up associating money with. This resulted in a win-win for the couple, who were then better positioned to work together. So, taking their early money lessons into account enabled a smoother approach to how they viewed money in their later years. This more in-depth look enables us to understand where our own and our partner's behaviour is coming from. The lessons we learn about money from our money-relationship blueprint stay with us our whole lives.

Your – and my – first money memory

The second question in Retiremeant Reflection 7 is an important one and relates to the early memories around money that you have. No matter how old you are, the reality is that for most of us, our first money memory is as clear as if it happened just yesterday. Decades can pass and still we can remember a money memory: a parent making a comment about money, a family argument over spending, a dispute around pocket money or the cost of replacing a lost toy.

Memories around money trigger associations we make with money, associations that impact the way we engage with money – even decades later. Here are a few examples of money memories from some of my clients:

- I was young when my father died; I experienced enormous fear that we would lose our house and not have a home.
- As a child, I was made aware that my family was not "well-to-do". Sometimes we even had to rely on charity handouts.
- From the age of eight, I would have to go on the tram on my own and do my mother's grocery shopping for her.
- I used to get a shilling pocket money as a child every so often. This was for me to buy the luxuries I wanted.
- I am a war-time child and so I experienced war-time rationing. One of my first memories around money was collecting the deposit money from returning glass bottles to my local café.

These first money memories are still part of how these clients feel about and engage with money, even if they are in their sixties or seventies. Does your first money memory still affect your relationship with money today?

I have made reference to the fact that to my mind, my father controlled my mother using money. It seemed to me that he felt he had the right to do so. Looking back at it from my perspective now, I believe that this behaviour was based on my father's insecurities: he felt that if he was in charge of the money, he would always be needed; I just didn't understand this at the time. I observed this as a child and, from a young age, promised myself that I would be successful and be financially independent. This was so that nobody could bully me. Even though my husband is generous with his money, my years of being out of the workplace while raising children left me feeling insecure. I felt vulnerable because of my childhood money memory which, even though just a belief – as most of what we hold to is – I saw it as a reality.

When you behave in a certain way with regard to money, ask yourself if this behaviour is based on reality, or a belief.

Face to face

Mary is a client who, for many years, was driven by a desire for success. This, by her own admission, was to heal an experience she had at sixteen. As a teenager, she had been enrolled at a prestigious school. Even though her school catered to families with money, Mary didn't have the money that the other students had. Her family couldn't afford the expensive, trendy outfits that the other girls wore. This translated into Mary having to wear her school uniform to a school social function – when all the other girls were arriving in casual wear. This was a pivotal moment for Mary. She felt scorned and alone. So, she made up her mind there and then: never again would she allow herself to feel less than good enough if she could help it. Based on this money memory, she built a life of success in the business world.

Our meeting and chatting about her money memory could never have changed that memory. But accessing the memory helped Mary to accept that it was just a belief rooted in one particular experience – and that she could, in fact, take on a less pressurised role within the company, still doing what she loved doing, and build for herself fulfilling activities outside of work. But she needed to acknowledge that money memory in order to begin her journey towards feeling secure in reducing her work pace – and still feel successful.

The financial fall-out

The third question you answered in the Retiremeant Reflection 7 had to do with the people in your life affected by the financial decisions you make. If your planner doesn't know who those people are, he or she may be quick to make assumptions about who they might be. A lot has been written about the so-called "sandwich generation". Many of my clients are financially responsible for their ageing parents as well as their growing children. They are monetarily overcommitted as they serve two generations in need. A scenario like this can put immense pressure on anybody's retirement savings. Your financial commitments are pertinent to your financial life plan, and so be sure to share information like this so that your plan can be as realistic as possible. Do you have siblings who need your help? Do you have a special-needs child or grandchild? These commitments will push your costs up. All these people and areas of concern need to be taken into account when you do your planning.

Planners from your past

The fourth question you answered tapped into your experience with financial planners. What past experiences stand out? And how have these experiences impacted how you engage with your current planner? Sadly, in the financial industry, too many clients have had bad experiences with financial planners in the past. This stems from the legacy of planners whose earnings were based only on commission. This resulted in a commission-driven incentive to sell a particular product – sometimes an inappropriate one – to a client. This lack of client-centric advice has left many retirees with uncertainty and cynicism. And understandably so.

But that is not necessarily how things are now. The industry today is far more regulated – and much more professional. In Chapter 10, I have included a list of what to look for when choosing a financial planner with whom to entrust your life savings in retirement. Start to set the boundaries in your mind and lay the foundation of what you expect from your relationship with your planner from the beginning. Be open to the role of a financial planner; he or she can add enormous value to your life by offering an objective view of a situation – the emotions around money can often cloud our judgement. It is much easier to navigate forward when you have some kind of support when making detailed decisions of what retirement money to put where.

Going forward financially

Essential to going forward is taking a good look at where you are in life – the principles and standards that are important to you. This will set you up to be satisfied with your plan of choice because you will have clarified your priorities and made sure that your financial decisions align with your principles.

RETIREMEANT REFLECTION 8 What does your money mean?

Understanding your principles around money is essential for the journey you are on. Here are some questions to help you better understand yours.

1. If you had all the money you would ever need, what would you do differently with your life?

....

....

....

....

....

2. With the above answer in mind then, what do you think your money truly represents to you?

....

....

....

....

....

3. Are there any investments you would avoid as a matter of princip e? List them here and say why you feel they do not resonate with you.

....

....

....

....

....

4. Do you have specific expectations of a financial planner? If so, what are they?

....

....

....

....

....

Download a free template of this Retiremeant Reflection by visiting www.retiremeant.co.za

Let's unpack some of your responses to these questions in the paragraphs that follow.

Face to face

Barbara, a mother to two children aged five and eight, came to see me. She wanted to make an investment as she wanted to buy a holiday home, having fond memories from her childhood of happy times at her family's holiday home. Now her life was very different, but she believed that if she had a holiday home, she would have more quality time with her children. Making this investment meant that Barbara needed to work much longer hours to be able to afford it.

At this point, most financial planners would set about advising on an investment to realise Barbara's dream. But I delved deeper. Barbara's mindset shifted when we chatted and she decided that working longer hours for this holiday home would in fact result in less quality time with her children while they still needed her. Instead, she reduced her work hours and decided to rent holiday homes, enabling her to spend more time with her children.

So, as the first question asked of you: if you had all the money you would ever need, what would you do differently with your life? Remember Retiremeant Truth No. 2 on page 19? Asking yourself these questions helps you think out of the box. Sometimes those answers are a warning to us that we are not living life to the full. Exploring life in this way enables hidden dreams to be expressed and explored. Think back to our Disney dreaming. My experience is that clients often don't allow themselves to think big because they believe they can't afford to. So, go back and answer this question from your heart before your head tells you it is not possible. Then let your planner help you to find a way to make at least some of your dreams – if not all of them – a reality.

The meaning of money

You've spent some time thinking through what money truly represents to you. For many of us, it represents success. But go a little deeper. What then might *success* mean to you? Perhaps it means financial independence and security so that you can enjoy a lifestyle that is healthy, fun, rewarding and sustainable. Or perhaps you plan to use your money to leave a legacy, something that is close to your heart. It is important to explore this area and put money in its proper place in your life as an enabler, opening doors to give you the life you want – whatever that may be. Remember Truth No 4 on page 22? Be master of your money.

Here are examples of what some clients had to say after answering the second question on what money represents to them:

- Money represents freedom from the insecurities that I carry from my past.
- Money is a way to enjoy the rest of my life with my husband.
- Money is something that allows me to be generous towards others.
- Money is not the "be-all and end-all" but it helps me to live the lifestyle that I do.
- I need to have enough so as never to be financially dependent on anyone else.
- It's important for me to have enough so that when I decide to stop working, I can do whatever I want for the rest of my life.

Avoiding and expecting

So, are there any investments you would avoid as a matter

of principle? Imagine if you had lost a close family member to alcoholism and subconsciously you blamed some of this on alcoholic beverage manufacturers. Imagine then that your planner bought you shares in one of these companies. That fit would not be right for you. Thinking through questions such as these and bringing such issues to your planner keeps trust intact and prevents decisions such as these from being taken.

Whether you realise it or not, you will have expectations of that planner. Start then to establish for yourself what those expectations are. This is so that he or she can help manage those expectations to make sure that you are not disappointed if he or she can't live up to them. The reason most clients leave their financial planners is that their expectations are not met. Are you looking for a financial planner to get you realistic returns on your money? Are you looking for someone to support you through life's opportunities and challenges? Express that.

Most people are worried that they won't have enough money in retirement and that they will run out of money. Is this a fact or a perception? Many clients I work with were poor as children and no amount of money seems to be able to take that fear of poverty away. But having a financial planner or a partner to discuss this with helps keep the fear in perspective. Visiting – and sometimes challenging – those early-established money relationships can go a long way to dealing with that fear. I cannot emphasise the point enough: first money memories can affect decisions you make for the rest of your life. Are your expectations of retirement that you should then never spend what you have? You have to get out of the mindset that when in retirement, you need to save your money. You have been saving for this season called *retirement*. You've been saving for decades! Now the money you've worked so hard to save must work for you; it must provide you with an income. Buying into this new way of thinking can be difficult. But this is the *very* time of your life that you have been saving for.

Do you have an expectation of extensive overseas travel during your retirement years? Where did that expectation come from? And why overseas? Delve some more. Are you after a particular type of experience? Probably. But don't be closed to the fact that local travel can give you this too. Be open to changing how you see things. Travel literally – and figuratively – with new eyes, opening yourself to new experiences, altering the kaleidoscope just a little.

> *"The real voyage of discovery consists not in seeking new landscapes, but in having new eyes."*
>
> French novelist, Marcel Proust

Now that you have a clearer sense of what money means to you, you can continue planning for your retirement. You can't change your history; you can't change your past. You can, however, be more conscious of your relationship with money and what it represents to you. Put money in its proper place before you turn that kaleidoscope a fraction – from money to *time*. Yes, we are going to look at the 168 hours a week that we have as retirees. We may not all have the same amount of money. But we have the same amount of time. How we make use of that time becomes the next part of our journey in planning for our retirement. Here we look in more detail at the next part of the process of transition through which you are going. Are you starting to see the world in a different way?

Your second half is the
perfect time to carve a
significant – and not
just successful –
life for yourself.

CHAPTER 6

From Money to Meaning

"The kaleidoscope can actually be used as a metaphor for life: with each twist in the cosmic universe we will experience a change in the settings of our lives. We adapt and live with the change as we adjust our vision to the new pattern of life set before us."

Writer, speaker and business owner, Michelle Beckham-Corbin

The next part of the process is looking at the transition you are going through in retirement.

In principle, retirement affords you more time for living. You or your spouse may have spent decades dedicating vast amounts of time to the building of a career or to the growing of a business. In this second half, that time is your own. You have 168 hours of it a week; that's definite. Now that you have this time, what do you do with it?

RETIREMENT TRANSITIONS

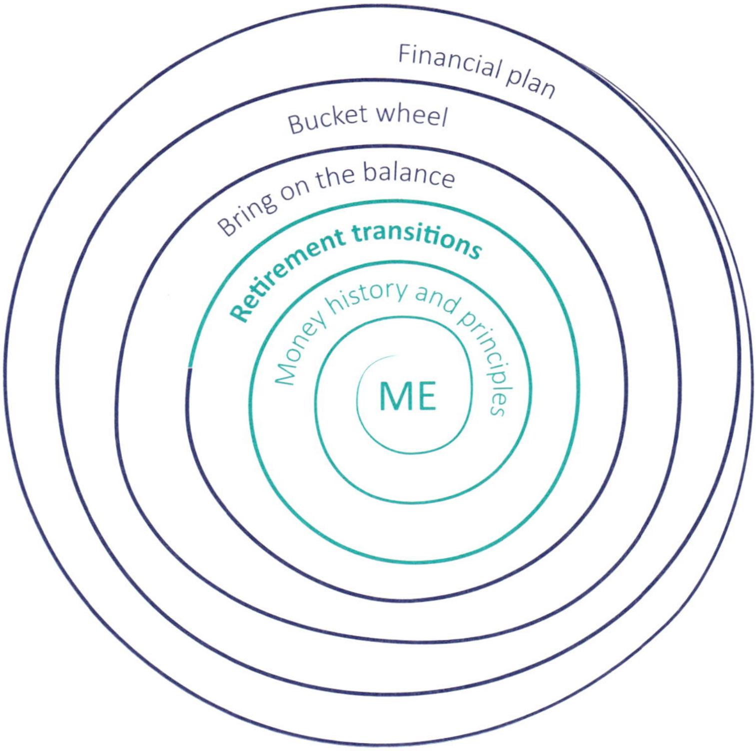

Retire *to* and not *from*

Time is a funny thing. Sometimes we appreciate it most when something threatens it: a health scare may take us back to basics, make us reassess our lives and look at how we have spent our time. A divorce or the loss of a loved one may spark a new direction in how we use the time left to us. That crossroads moment, often prompted by an inner voice that poses pertinent and personal questions, is what many retirees feel they have reached when they're on the brink of their new life in retirement.

I can't tell you how important it is to listen to that voice. That voice will ask questions and provide answers, tell you things about yourself that you may know only on a subconscious level. Being able to hear that inner voice takes introspective work. I believe that as human beings, we already have all the answers we need for a meaningful life. They're right inside of us. But we do need to be open to doing the work, to go on a proverbial journey if you will, in order to hear them. If we aren't open to hearing that inner voice – and then making the necessary changes – we face the possibility of a disappointing retirement.

"If the still, small voice is speaking to you now, do not look for reasons to ignore it. There will always be reasons to stay where you are."

CABLE TV PIONEER AND SOCIAL ENTREPRENEUR, BOB BUFORD

In this self-auditing process, I have found author Bob Buford's work of enormous value: he looks at retirement being a time in your life that affords you the opportunity to transition from what you have deemed "success" in your career to the opportunity to be "significant" in this new life phase. Buford's *Success to Significance* terminology is the inspiration for this chapter's title, "From Money to Meaning". Bob makes use of the term "halftime" (in fact, *Halftime* is the title of one of his books), reflected in the graph that follows, to signify the watershed moment that a transition into retirement – and a potential shift from success to significance – can be. Yes, the transition into retirement, as evidenced by the "halftime" mark depicted in the graphic which follows, can usher in a time of uncertainty. But it can be – and so often is – a time of review and reflection. And it's the perfect time to carve a significant, and not just successful, life for yourself.

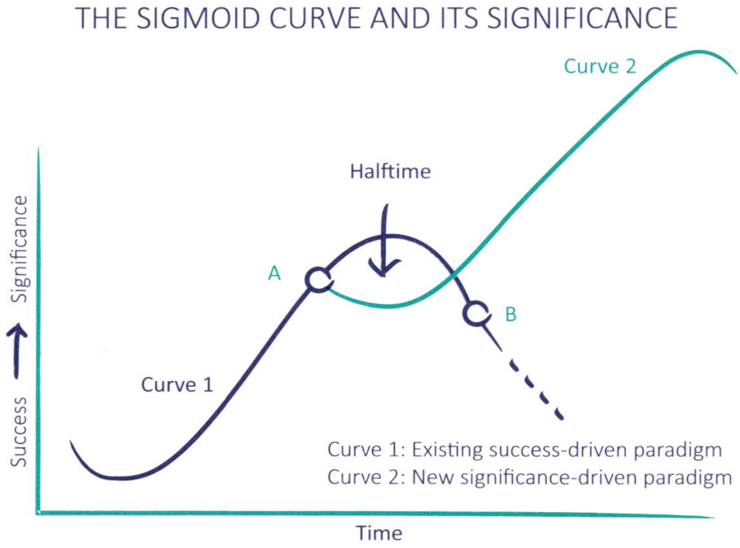

Adapted from Charles Handy (1994). *The Empty Raincoat: Making Sense of the Future.* Random House Adult Trade Publisher Group

This graph sets the tone for the possibilities of how life in retirement could play itself out. The Sigmoid Curve, reflected here, has been used by many to make the case for significant ongoing change. The graph depicts, if you will, how humans can reinvent themselves with an initial period of learning followed by a time of growth and development. What the graph also depicts is that there are two possible curves. How you respond to that inner voice – ignore or listen to – will take you on one of two possible journeys.

Curve 1 depicts your success-driven life phase that you have been in up until now. In the first half of life, we are very much focused on doing our best to advance our careers, provide for our families and instil the beliefs and values we hold dear in our children. During our first half, life has a lot to do with achieving, earning, gaining and learning. Most of us make strides in these areas by getting an education, entering the workforce, buying a house, starting a family – and earning enough money to provide for our needs and a few wants as well as setting goals and advancing towards them.

Then, at Point A on the graph, we reach a watershed moment and it becomes time for us to look at making some changes – especially if we want to ensure that there is meaning in our retirement. Point A is when we think about what we would like our retirement to look like. Making no adjustments at the "halftime" mark will take you down to Point B, which represents a less-than-ideal dip towards a possibly less significant second half.

If we go down this curve, it is very hard to get back up. Imagine that you are told that you are a high-risk candidate for a heart attack – that you need to make changes to your diet and that you have to manage your stress levels for the sake of your health. Imagine not listening to that advice. And then having a heart attack. Now imagine only being able to do half the things you used to do: your limited physical ability, your restricted diet. This is how not taking a watershed moment seriously can play itself out. The result? Experiencing a downhill curve from which it is impossible to bounce back.

In order to create a life of more meaning, it is important to do some personal exploring. In the life-planning meetings I run with my clients, I encourage them to find a quiet place and, with pen and paper, to give themselves time to work out what they want to do with their second halves. When you come to this moment in your own journey, remember that you have earned the choices that you are now making. I would imagine that you feel that, for far too long, many decisions have been made for you – and that you have done what others have expected from you. Perhaps you spent time developing strategic plans for your business or career? Well, now it is time to work on a strategic plan for you. Maybe your first half was spent nurturing children? Well, now you will be able to nurture *you*.

If you equated your life to a sports match of some sort, then, just as with a rugby match or game of soccer, "halftime" would be a time for taking stock, for looking back on what you have accomplished, for assessing what has worked – and what has not. If a strategy you were employing wasn't working, you, as coach, would make the necessary adjustments for a successful second-half experience. This is the time for new plans to be drawn up and integrated into your game plan. Many times, an excellent second half – and indeed an excellent game – depends on what happens at the "halftime" mark. In my life-planning meetings, I refer to this as your parallel life, which is pictured at "halftime". This is the time for you to decide how you want your life to look – and to redesign it accordingly.

CHARLES HANDY: THE AGE OF PARADOX

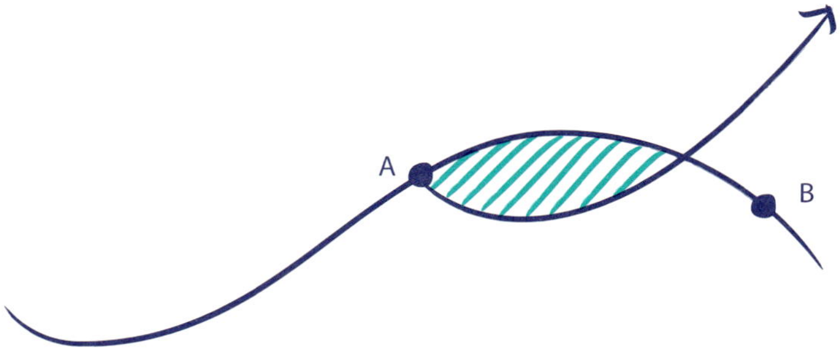

Adapted from Charles Handy (1994). *The Empty Raincoat: Making Sense of the Future.* Random House Adult Trade Publisher Group

Making the "halftime" changes we need to might not always be possible all at once. But if we start making small adjustments slowly, this parallel life graph soon starts shifting upwards and before we know it, we are living a healthier – and happier – life. The concept of retirement is no different. Research shows, for example, that if you don't start a hobby before you retire, chances are you won't start one afterwards. So, set up parallel interests that can come into play when your work hours reduce or cease. Don't be scared of taking these steps. Keep a positive attitude here: it's essential to see this as an adventure, an opportunity to fulfil some of your as yet unrealised dreams. Don't wait until you're too old or too tired. Embrace the change; embrace the challenge. So, sign up for those dancing classes you've always wanted to do; share your photographs with the world instead of hiding them away; write that book you've been too scared to start; complete that degree you never had the opportunity to; spend time with your grandchildren.

Making small, positive changes to your life will increase your chance of having something to retire *to* instead of waking up one morning to find yourself retired *from* a job – and having nothing to fill the now available hours that work once occupied.

RETIREMEANT REFLECTION 9 Are you up for it?

Consider the questions below and answer them in as much detail as possible. The goal of these exercises is to make this next chapter of your life an upward curve.

1. How are you feeling at the moment? What major transitions are you on the verge of making right now?

....

....

....

....

....

2. Do you have a clear plan for dealing with these feelings or transitions in order for Curve 2 to slope upwards for you?

....

....

....

....

....

3. Detail some of the aspects of your plan or feelings.

....

....

....

....

....

4. If your curve dips down, what do you think you can you do to regain energy, vision and momentum in the face of this?

....

....

....

....

....

Download a free template of this Retiremeant Reflection by visiting www.retiremeant.co.za

Face to face

One couple, Geoff and Helga, found themselves in just this situation. Helga was 58 and was successful in her career at the law firm at which she worked. However, she couldn't see herself being in that career until the retirement age of 65. It was stressful and demanding of her time and Helga felt that she had something else to offer the world. In her personal explorations, she decided to sign up for a life-coaching programme – as well as a gardening course! Moreover, she decided to reconfigure her career so that she would only work three days a week – as a life-coach and not a lawyer – and then, for the remaining two days, bring creativity back into her life by working in her gardens, attending courses and visiting beautiful estates around the country. Friday would be when Helga would prioritise painting, a pastime she last did 30 years previously, as well as seeing people who were precious to her. This way, her life – and the reconfiguration of her week – kept her connected to herself and others.

And so, I encourage you to share your thoughts and dreams with your significant other so that he or she can support you as you integrate these changes into your life.

"Twenty years from now you will be more disappointed by the things that you didn't do than by the ones you did do. So throw off the bowlines. Sail away from the safe harbor. Catch the trade winds in your sails. Explore. Dream. Discover."

American author, Mark Twain

Face to face

Bruce and Sue sat opposite me. They had come to see if they had enough money to retire. Bruce was 59, and his job, which he did on a contractual basis, had come to an end. This had been unexpected and, as a result, he felt at a loss. His and his wife's initial response was to move to their holiday house at the coast. Further investigations revealed that finances were not an issue. But what kind of life were Bruce and Sue retiring to? Sue seemed prepared for a life change such as this: she hadn't done formal work and had moved countries often – wherever Bruce's job had taken them. This meant that she was practised at making new friends, developing hobbies to keep her challenged, finding charities with which to get involved – as well as churches for community connections. But things were different for Bruce. He had dedicated his life to his work. Now what was he going to fill his time with? He did not make friends easily – and he was far too energetic to not replace his work with something meaningful.

Over the course of the next few months, which Bruce described as very difficult – he even admitted that my challenging him to think through things made him not like me very much – he did introspective work, exploring places he had never been before and spent a lot of time thinking about his parallel life. In fact, Bruce embraced this process like no other client I've had. He engaged fully in his own journey and came up with a plan. As a result, Bruce is no longer despondent. Instead he feels like he is in control of his life. He has been approached to do contract work in Africa, which he has taken up. Sue enjoys being at home and has a full life living in an estate. Bruce works for three weeks at a time and then comes home for three weeks. He loves travelling around the country and playing golf in his three weeks off.

RETIREMEANT REFLECTION 10 To work or not to work?

Taking some time to answer the following questions can prove very helpful when you are considering a new career or changes to your existing one.

1. Think back to a time when you were most happy in your career. Why do you think you were so content?

....

....

....

....

....

2. What are you really passionate about? What makes you feel alive?

....

....

....

....

....

3. What would you say are your core values?

....

....

....

....

....

4. What are your greatest strengths?

....

....

....

....

....

5. Is there something that you could add to your life right now that you believe would give it more meaning? What would that be?

....

....

....

....

....

6. Take a moment to think about this. In what way do you believe your first-half experience could be seen as a foundation for something significant in your second half?

....

....

....

....

....

Download a free template of this Retiremeant Reflection by visiting www.retiremeant.co.za

Sometimes, "halftime" considerations involve a rethink of where you are positioned – not just personally but geographically. Wanting to live in a different town or part of the country is not an uncommon consideration for people on the verge of retirement. Many clients, having lived in busy and traffic-ridden cities, yearn for a peaceful life at the coast or a future in a smaller and safer space. If this is what you desire, take a look one more time at the preceding graph above. Where are you positioned on the Sigmoid Curve, on page 78 time-wise? What plans do you need to put in place for your parallel life? I have seen many clients successfully integrate into new towns and social circles with the correct consideration and planning.

Face to face

Jessica and Paul wanted to relocate from Johannesburg to the coast when they retired. They were advised not to sell everything on retirement and make the sudden shift. Instead, they bought a holiday home at the coast and over a period of ten years spent more and more time there. This gradual physical – and psychological – shift enabled them, over time, to explore the area and make new friends, all in anticipation of when they would move there. Paul had been an airline pilot in his career. During those ten years, he bought a glider and a plane – and a hangar at the local airport so that he could continue his flying interests in his ultimate hometown. Putting this parallel life in place meant that Jessica and Paul had something to move to – and not just *from*.

RETIREMEANT REFLECTION 11 Where do you want to be?

If you are planning to relocate in your retirement years to a different city or part of the country, it is important to start building a parallel life for yourself in that area. If you are planning a geographical shift in time to come, spend some time considering these questions.

1. What town, city or area are you considering retiring to?

....

2. What do you believe this town or city offers you? Why are you drawn to this particular place?

....

....

....

....

3. How much time do you spend there at the moment? Can you increase your visits there in the months and years to come? As you think about this, consider honestly what it would be like to live there, and not just have a holiday there.

....

....

....

....

4. Explore some of the spaces you can that might enable you to meet people or be energised by different activities. These may include golf courses and country clubs, gyms, churches, recreational centres, art workshops, cooking schools, gardening schools. Write down three possible recreational areas you would be interested in tapping into and give yourself a deadline date (write it down) by which you need to have made contact with that organisation for informational or joining purposes. Ask to be put on a database or decide to follow a Facebook page to be kept informed – and on your next visit there, make sure you touch base with at least one of these groups.

....

....

....

....

Download a free template of this Retiremeant Reflection by visiting www.retiremeant.co.za

Even if a geographical shift isn't on the cards for you, a decision that most retirees face is whether to stay in their large family house or retire to a smaller residence; and if you do downsize, whether to move into a retirement estate or not. When it comes to retirement villages, people either love or hate the idea. There is no middle ground here and I find that people tend to have very strong views in this regard. You'll need to weigh up the pros and cons for yourself; speak to people who have made the move – and those who haven't – for their perspectives.

Here are some considerations when it comes to the retirement estate debate:

- People choose retirement estate living for the security it provides, with most estates offering 24-hour access control. Many couples also choose to move into a retirement estate together with the view that when one spouse dies, the surviving spouse will be settled in a safe community environment.
- Many estates offer a live-in frail care centre with the option of in-home nursing care. This might not seem necessary if you're 60, but when you are past 80, it may become an important consideration.
- One up – or down – side of estate living is the sense of community it provides. This type of lifestyle can give you many opportunities to make new friends and create the type of social connections that are essential to your sense of wellbeing in retirement.
- Estate living implies reduced maintenance costs. The typically smaller houses and communal gardens maintained by the estate enhance a stress-free lifestyle, an essential consideration for some in their second half.

- Whether you choose a new or established estate is also something to consider. An established estate allows you to assess building quality and infrastructure such as what levies are set at and how smoothly they are running. But a new estate offers you flexibility with regard to house design. Be sure, however, to check developer credentials.
- When it comes to financing your new house, different developments offer different ways of structuring your house purchase. Some use a life rights model (occupancy without ownership); others offer sectional title schemes; and some offer outright purchase models. These purchase schemes can be complex and may have pitfalls, so it is best to discuss the various options with your financial advisor.
- If you do decide to opt for estate living, put your name down early. You never think you are going to be "ready" to move into one of these places, and when you are ready, it's too late!

Whether your move into retirement is a geographical one or not, the most important move you can make is the upward move on your own personal Sigmoid Curve on page 78. I encourage you to consider the concept of the *Five Vitamin Cs* developed by Mitch Anthony to ensure that a move into your second half will indeed help your graph curve upwards (Curve 2). Here they are.

The Five Vitamin Cs

Vitamin C1: Connectivity

You might be tempted to consider moving away from your current city to a smaller, possibly coastal, town on retirement. Please let me caution you before you do. Unless you know the place well, you are setting yourself up to spend your remaining years in a space with no social connectivity. People who do this are essentially disconnecting from a major lifeline in the science of successful ageing. They are abandoning their often vast existing social networks for nothing more than a view of the sea.

Having said that, a common mistake retirees make is relocating to the place they've had fabulous holidays at in the past. A three-week holiday at the beach is very different from living there full time. The silence that surrounds your idyllic Karoo farmhouse can become deafening once you're living there permanently. You would be wise to spend some time doing thorough reconnaissance on the area you're planning to move to. Often clients have to decide whether or not to join children who have emigrated. This requires careful consideration. Discussion points include the priority of family, financial constraints and the possibility of children relocating again before they settle.

Many people disconnect themselves from important social networks when they retire and don't realise it until it's too late. Staying connected to people you love is essential to both your physical and mental wellbeing. This is never more crucial than when you head into retirement. Isolation and loneliness in retirement are very real threats and the solution is connectivity.

Vitamin C2: Challenge

Alzheimer research shows that being intellectually challenged and having regular taxation on our mental acuity literally staves off the degenerative processes leading to both Alzheimers disease and dementia. This research also concluded that as we hit our 50s and beyond, it is important to ensure that we have riddles to ponder, problems to solve and things to fix. The brain is a muscle that, like all muscles, atrophies without use.

Vitamin C3: Curiosity

Curiosity helps keep our minds ticking over and our bodies healthy. The role of mental alertness cannot be overestimated. It need not be formal education that you pursue; it can be something self-taught or some form of experiential learning. The important thing is to stay curious and be open to growing. Age is an uphill road. Learning tasks that demand mental alertness keep us on track. Rigorous mental function helps both to facilitate productivity in later years and to strengthen our need and desire to be active, which is turn affects our physical wellbeing.

Vitamin C4: Creativity

A creative soul looks at the shoreline and sees something new every day. This might help explain why BB King, now over 80, plays over 200 nights a year, and why Peter Drucker was able to write a business best seller in his 90s. Of course, you don't have to be renowned to be creative and to keep the powers of observation working. You just have to be curious, intrigued, expressive and intentional.

Vitamin C5: Charity

Studies continue to show the positive effects charitable living has on the quality and longevity of a person's life. Those who think about helping others often share their thoughts that giving in this way takes the focus off their own problems – as well as the degenerative effects of stress associated with self-preoccupation. Even if you didn't live a day longer because of charitable pursuits, you will no doubt live better.

RETIREMEANT REFLECTION 12 Are you taking your vitamins?

Based on what you have just read, take some time now and score yourself in each of the five areas. Circle the number most applicable to you in each case.

Connectivity

How connected am I to those people who energise me and are energised by me?

Not nearly enough — Some — Very much

1 2 3 4 5 6 7 8 9 10

Challenge

How much intellectual and physical challenge do I have in my daily life?

Not nearly enough — Some — Very much

1 2 3 4 5 6 7 8 9 10

Curiosity

How focused am I on growing and expanding my knowledge?

Not nearly enough — Some — Very much

1 2 3 4 5 6 7 8 9 10

Creativity

How much creativity/enjoyment do I have in my life?

Not nearly enough — Some — Very much

1 2 3 4 5 6 7 8 9 10

Charity

How much of myself (time, energy, resources) do I give toward helping others?

Not nearly enough — Some — Very much

1 2 3 4 5 6 7 8 9 10

If you score below 7 for any of the areas, perhaps consider what you can do to increase that score. Our next chapter will give you some ideas if you feel you are needing help. Remember: you are in the process of allowing the kaleidoscope colours to rearrange themselves as you aim to bring significance and balance to your life.

Download a free template of this Retiremeant Reflection by visiting www.retiremeant.co.za

Even though "halftime" can be a period of uncertainty and even discontent, choose to see it as a time to reflect on your life and what's important to you. And now that we have explored how to bring more meaning to your life, it is time to take a look at how balanced your life feels. How do these eight essential elements – working, learning, money, being healthy, playing, relationships, having a sense of purpose and giving back – play themselves out in your life? Even if this is the first time you've considered what you really want to do with your life – on your own terms – it's an exciting time. Now let's look at how balanced your life is and construct an action plan going forward.

"A journey of a thousand miles
begins with a single step."

CHINESE PROVERB

A rewarding retirement experience consists of a life in which the core areas are all engaged.

CHAPTER 7

The Balancing Act

"The world is your kaleidoscope, and the varying combinations of colours, which at every succeeding moment it presents to you are the exquisitely adjusted pictures of your ever-moving thoughts."

ENGLISH AUTHOR AND POET, JAMES ALLEN

Your life consists of many facets, some more important to you than others. Neglecting just one of them can have an effect on the others. For example, having excellent personal relationships would be of little value to you if your health were poor and you weren't able to fully enjoy the people in your life. That is why, in order to feel fulfilled in retirement, it's important that you consciously consider your current and future goals and then be deliberate about setting time aside for every area of your life.

When we are working full time, time is an incredibly scarce resource. For most of us, work occupies 40 or more hours out of our 168-hour week. And then we sleep for 56 hours of those anyway. The idea of having time to ourselves can seem absurd. It is for this reason that many of my clients cannot wait to retire. In short, they are tired and want down time.

No matter the age we are, achieving some sense of balance in life seems like a challenge, doesn't it? In an ideal world, if we were truly living life in balance, we wouldn't even be retiring. In our accumulating years, we are so busy trying to save from what we earn, provide a home for our family and educate our children that we feel compelled to put as much time into work as we can. Now, at the point of retirement, many of us are faced with having to leave our work and rethink those 168 hours per week. When we have them, what will we do with them?

BRING ON THE BALANCE

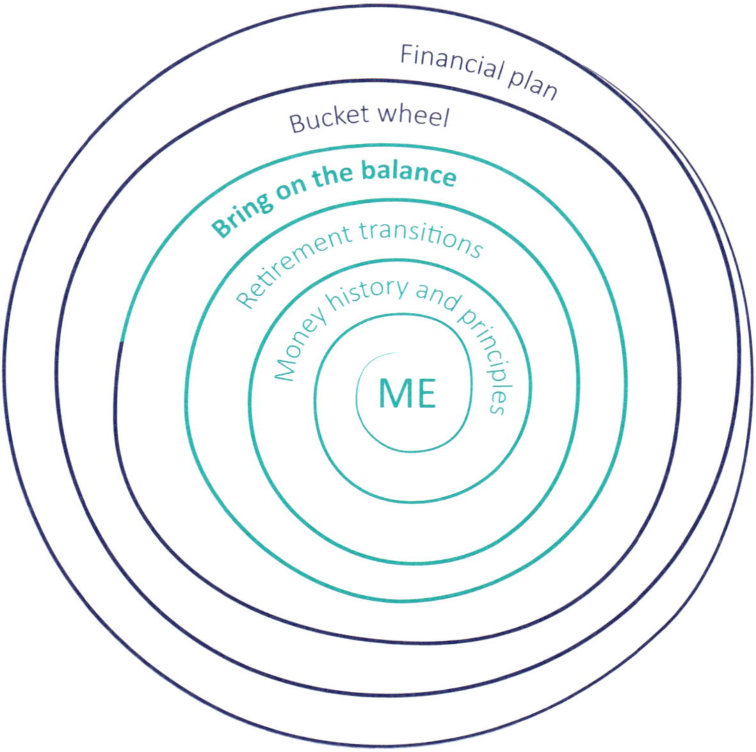

The work I do with my clients has made me more convinced than ever that finding some sense of balance in retirement is absolutely essential. And it's a great place to start when working out for yourself exactly what it is that you are going to retire to. So let's get started on the process and take a look at how balanced you feel your life is right now.

Eight essentials for balanced beings

Imagine looking through a kaleidoscope. Now visualise the array of colours and images transforming themselves as you rotate the tube. The patterns of a kaleidoscope are repeated, segment by segment – each section is the same size and shape as the one next to it. To my mind, balance in retirement should look exactly like this, the areas of your life moving as shapes in perfect harmony with one another.

A rewarding retirement experience consists of a life in which the core areas of that life are all engaged. Focus too much on playing and the rest of your world falls apart. Obsess too much over money and your relationships will suffer. These lessons are true of life – and not just of retirement, right? I see balance as comprising eight essential elements that, working in harmony with one another, set you up for a rewarding retirement. These are: Work, Give Back, Relationships, Money, Learn, Health, Purpose and Play. It is almost impossible for each area to be perfectly balanced in relation to the others. But what *is* important – and *essential* – is to be engaged, to some degree, in each area itself.

Take a look at the *Life in Balance Wheel* that follows. It shows, pictorially, the eight areas I have just mentioned – all of which, I believe, contribute to a contented life in retirement. Even though money is represented – and rightly so – it is merely a tool for achieving your life goals. Balance in life comes from the interplay between all eight elements.

LIFE IN BALANCE WHEEL

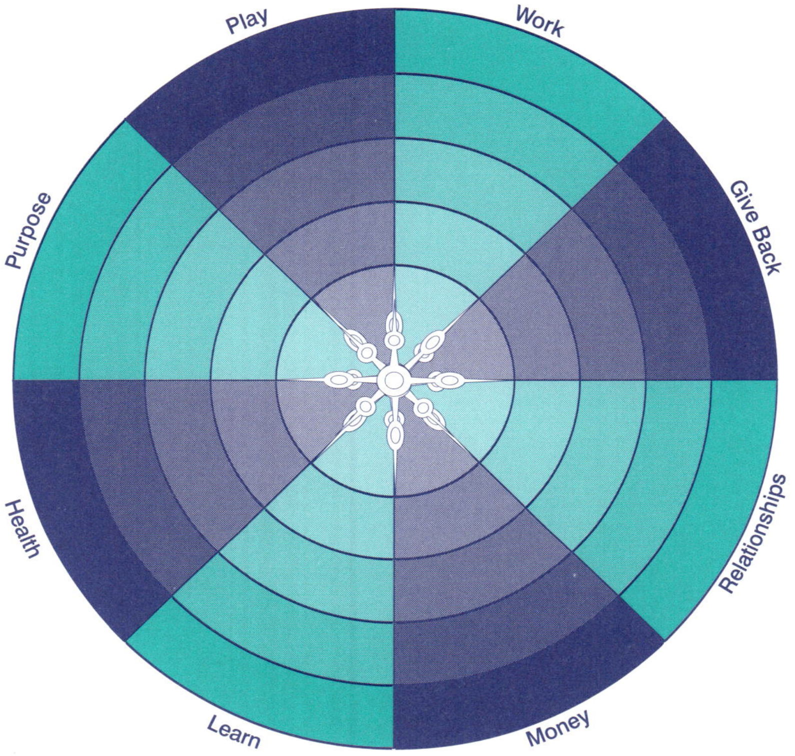

Retirement is an exciting life phase. It's an opportunity to achieve your as yet unfulfilled dreams and goals. Yes, some things are less enjoyable than others: is a visit to your cardiologist as exciting as a visit to Venice? No, but it's no less important. Work is key to who you have been and will, no doubt, still have a role to play in your life going forward. Giving back – to people, institutions or to society in general – is an integral part of your humanity. And relationships? Well, none of us exists as an island, and being cognisant of the people in our world is essential to our engaging on this planet – as is the idea of play where we get to enjoy the lives we have with the people we love.

And like it or not, money is important. Without it we cannot live. This means that mastering who we are in relation to money is an essential life skill. Having a sense of purpose and learning in life are two imperatives when it comes to our evolving as human beings. And what point is there to *any* of this if your body isn't well enough to truly live in your life? Your health is vital. And so, your retirement is essentially a relationship between these eight equally important aspects of life, each of them as vital to your wellbeing as the other.

How balanced is your life?

Before we spend some time honing in on these eight essentials, we need to see where you are on this proverbial *Wheel of Balance*. How do you fare? Are there areas of your life that you should focus on for a more enriching existence?

Here's a very simple test that can give you a good indication of where you place yourself. It will take no more than ten minutes and has been designed, in an easy-to-visualise format, to show you how balanced your life feels to you right now. Consider taking this same test in, say, six months' time. That way you can evaluate whether your levels of fulfilment – and your sense of overall balance – have improved. The results displayed in the Retiremeant Reflection that follows will offer you a visual representation of where your mind is at and will help you to identify which areas of your life might need a bit of work.

RETIREMEANT REFLECTION 13 How balanced are you?

For this exercise you will answer one question pertaining to each of the eight essential elements your life consists of. Read each question and then give yourself a fulfilment rating out of five (see the Fulfilment Scale below). Colour in on the Wheel of Balance diagram provided on page 102 according to your rating in that particular area of your life as you see it currently. Seeing it in the colour associated with that area leaves a much stronger representation in your memory.

The aim is not necessarily to get a 5/5 fulfilment rating for each of the areas. It's to see how balanced one area is in relation to the others. How closely will your final image represent a circle, a wheel? Be honest with where you are at or the exercise becomes meaningless; this exercise is for you to see where you are so that you can work on ideas on how to improve your balance.

The Balance Test

Fulfilment Scale:

1. Completely unfulfilled
2. Unfulfilled
3. Indifferent
4. Fulfilled
5. Completely fulfilled

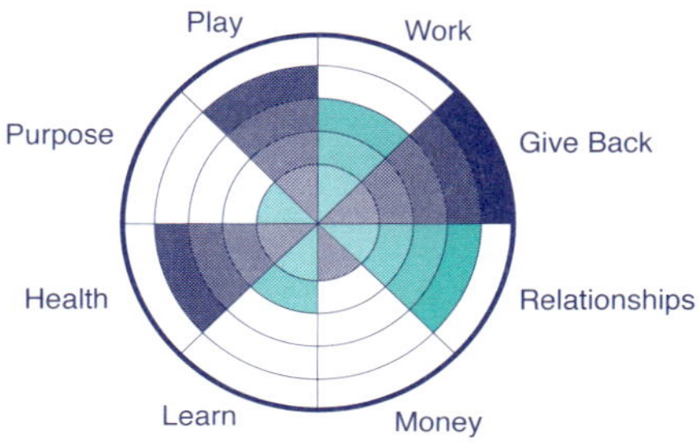

Example completed Wheel of Balance

RETIREMEANT REFLECTION 13 How balanced are you?

Segment questions

Money: Do you have enough money to live the lifestyle you want in retirement? Is money your master or your servant?

Purpose: To what extent do you believe that you have discovered your greater purpose? And are you living – or do you see yourself living – your life in retirement in accordance with this greater purpose?

Work: Whether you are engaged in a formal work situation or not, how useful do you feel? To what degree do you feel that you are making a contribution in some way?

Health: How would you rate your health? Are you confident that you are in good enough health that your lifestyle is not hindered or that you will not be a burden to anyone else?

Give back: How much of yourself (time, energy, resources) do you give back to your community or to causes close to your heart?

Learn: How would you score yourself when it comes to learning new things? Do you make a conscious effort to learn new things and keep yourself mentally stimulated?

Play: How much enjoyment do you have in your life? How often do you laugh? How much time do you set aside to play?

Relationships: How much of your time would you say you spend on nurturing the relationships that are important to you? How significant a role do relationships play in your world?

RETIREMEANT REFLECTION 13 How balanced are you?

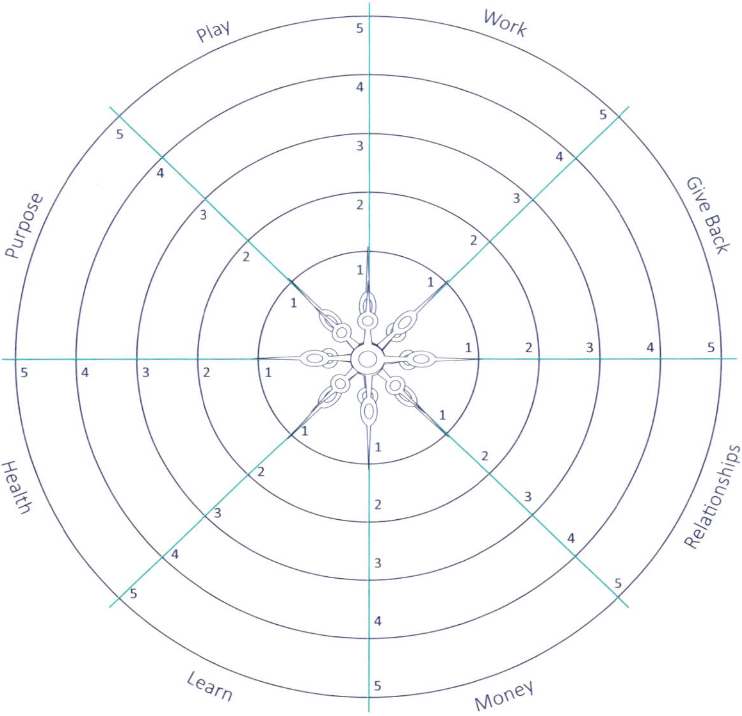

Download a free template of this Retiremeant Reflection by visiting www.retiremeant.co.za

You will no doubt have discovered that some areas of your life score more highly than others. Set aside some time and energy to focus on those low scores and to explore what is needed for optimum balance in your world. You know where you stand today. Now the question is: where do you want to be tomorrow? See this season as an opportunity to re-establish equilibrium by making time for those areas in your life you could not focus on during your more focused and high-pressure career years.

Having completed your *Wheel of Balance* will make you aware of the areas in your life that require attention. The next step is to evaluate what is – and what isn't – working in each of these areas. This will help you bring more balance to your life. Identifying the gaps will also give you direction when formulating your goals. Your life will never be perfectly in balance, but striving for that balance is important. Each of these life areas is connected to each other. It is very difficult to compartmentalise your life, and part of your journey is to see how one area affects another.

Our next Retiremeant Reflection offers you a way to put thought to paper and is an effective means of figuring things out. With both the objectives and the obstacles you face clear in your mind, you will be better positioned to give yourself the headspace to strategise. Don't just focus on the areas that feel out of balance for you; we are all quick to self-criticise. Make sure you celebrate areas of your life that *are* working well. It's just as important to recognise what *is* working as well as what is *not*.

RETIREMEANT REFLECTION 14 What's working?

Money

What's working?	What needs work?

Purpose

What's working?	What needs work?

Health

What's working?	What needs work?

Give Back

What's working?	What needs work?

Learn

What's working?	What needs work?

Play

What's working?	What needs work?

Relationships

What's working?	What needs work?

Work

What's working?	What needs work?

Download a free template of this Retiremeant Reflection by visiting www.retiremeant.co.za

This exercise is a very important piece of our retirement life plan. What it does for us is to put in place the foundation of what our life in retirement, to a large degree, is going to look like. This forms the framework, in fact, of what you are going to be doing in retirement. In the next chapter, we'll explore each segment of life in more detail and I will share with you some of my clients' stories, ideas, inspirations and insights. I hope that some of these will help motivate you to dream even bigger dreams for your life.

"Every man has within himself a continent of undiscovered character. Happy is he who proves the Columbus of his soul."

GERMAN AUTHOR, JOHANN WOLFGANG VON GOETHE

It doesn't really matter what you do at the end of the day. What matters is that what you do resonates with who you are.

CHAPTER 8

Bring on the Balance

"Our days are a kaleidoscope. Every instant a change takes place in the contintents. New harmonies, new contrasts, new combinations of every sort."

American speaker and social reformer, Henry Ward Beecher

It is often at this point in my clients' retirement plan journey that I see their body language start to change. This is where they start to get excited. Shoulders go back and eyes start to sparkle; ideas start to flow. I teasingly remind them that they are not meant to be comparing themselves to the Oprah Winfreys and the Richard Bransons of the world, but rather to respect what excites them in their own journey and not to worry about what others think. Isn't that one of the advantages of getting older? That we are less worried about what others think of us? I am not joking when I tell you that I have clients who have found their passions in life in areas that you wouldn't expect a person to: one client looks after orphan donkeys, would you believe? Another collects key rings from around the world! It does not matter what you do. What matters is that what you do resonates with who you are. I have learnt that there is something out there for everyone. You just need to find what that something is.

Let's continue the next part of our journey by exploring some insights into the eight essential areas you have spent some time looking at in relation to your life.

1. Work

Work is an essential part of feeling productive as a human being and, if you stop working permanently, it will be more than a salary and a schedule you'll be giving up. Guaranteed, the euphoria of not having to get up for work every day will wear off – and you'll find yourself with more time on your hands than you know what to do with – because there is much more to work and the impact that it has on who you are than you realise.

This season – scary as it can be – is also the ideal time for structuring your life as you want to, going forward. You don't necessarily have to stop working. You may need to continue earning an income or you may choose to work because you love what you do. This season is all about exploring the possibility of living and working differently. That could mean full-time or part-time work, consulting, volunteering or pursuing something completely new altogether. The goal should be being able to fit work into life, rather than trying to squeeze life into work. You might, after decades of hard work, want to opt for a traditional retirement and not work at all. Knowing what you enjoy and value about your career is a good place to start. But the why, what, where – and when – will be specific to you.

Work can be defined as a meaningful and productive engagement. For that, you can collect a material or an emotional pay-off – or both. Whether you are being paid or not, you need to feel that you are still useful and relevant. The idea is to move away from the idea of a "job" to something that gives you a sense of direction, accomplishment and worth. Work is about so much more than a salary. Work gives you a sense of usefulness. More and more retirees are opting never to fully retire; instead, they are restructuring their work lives. So explore what it is that you enjoy – or enjoyed – about your job and what will bring meaning to your life in retirement. Preparation is key here; waiting until you retire to start thinking about what you want to do makes for a lot of stress! Do the introspective work now. The questions that follow can be a powerful means of checking in with yourself:

RETIREMEANT REFLECTION 15 Check in with yourself

What are my greatest strengths and core values?

....

....

....

What am I really passionate about?

....

....

....

What makes me come alive?

....

....

....

What on earth would give my life meaning?

....

....

....

In what way was my first-half experience a foundation for something more significant in my second half?

....

....

....

Create a "love it-loathe it" list regarding your career and make sure your new job contains more "love it" elements.

The success of this exercise hinges on acknowledging that you know the answers already regarding your passions and the direction you should take – it is a matter of making time and creating silence to listen to that inner voice.

Download a free template of this Retiremeant Reflection by visiting www.retiremeant.co.za

Face to face

Michael and Sabrina came to see me recently. Michael, the CEO of a listed firm, was facing retirement. Sabrina was worried about how Michael would adjust to his new life as he had worked extremely long hours and was someone whose sense of identity was wrapped up in his work. Michael began his journey by exploring the questions we've just looked at. Did he want to stay in his career? Or did he want a complete change? Michael had three options: to stay at his company in a less stressful position with a salary drop; to start his own business in a similar line given that his knowledge of Africa in the context of his profession was unique; or to retire and "give back" by donating his time to an organisation.

After looking honestly at his answers, Michael concluded that opening his own business might make him money but would also tie him down, something that would prevent him from exploring other areas in life. The "give back" option in his particular industry implied the stresses of working with various government departments. So Michael chose to remain at his company. He dropped his work load to four days a week, took a pay cut and added a mentoring element to what he did. Michael now helps prepare other near-retirees for the transition into retirement and has found a work dynamic that suits his life.

2. Give back

Giving back is a state of mind and a way of life. Giving back is not limited to charity work. It has everything to do with the impact you want to make on the world, the legacy you want to leave behind. What does giving back look like to you? It could mean volunteering at your favourite charity. But it could also be mentoring or tutoring – or something as simple as recycling, giving a meal to a homeless child or developing the spirit of generosity in your world. This can play itself out in big ways or in small ways. A big way? Arranging a charity fundraiser. A small way? Teaching your grandson how to ride a bike.

"… to leave the world a bit better, whether by a healthy child, a garden patch or a redeemed social condition; to know even one life has breathed easier because you have lived. This is to have succeeded."

AMERICAN ESSAYIST, RALPH WALDO EMERSON

Living in a time of global change means that you should also be increasingly concerned about the environment and what kind of world you are leaving behind for your children and grandchildren. You have a responsibility to do as much as you can to ensure that you are creating a sustainable future for those who come after you. People often think that their contribution is too little and won't go far enough towards make a real difference in the world – that picking up a piece of litter here or closing a dripping tap there is of little consequence. But that is just not true. With 40-odd million people in South Africa alone – let alone the rest of the world – the actions of enlightened individuals are exactly what it will take to change the world we live in. The environment is the universe's gift to us: it provides for us, bestowing upon us immense beauty and pleasure. Ask yourself if you are doing enough to repay the favour. So, look beyond yourself and make a difference in this world.

"Society grows great when old men plant trees whose shade they shall never sit in."

GREEK PROVERB

Giving to others is the greatest gift we can give to ourselves. This is because happiness comes from giving – and not from getting. If you bring happiness to others, you can't stop yourself from feeling happy too. No, this is not your motive for giving back but it is certainly one of the rewards. Being charitable doesn't have to cost a lot. It doesn't have to cost anything at all, in fact. And it shouldn't be a chore. It is simply how you choose to make a difference. Whether your contribution is large or small, whenever you make a difference in the life of someone else, you are giving back. So choose to enrich your life by creating today what you want to be remembered for tomorrow. Give back in a way that resonates with you; there's no point in volunteering at the SPCA if you don't love animals. Play to your strengths: if you have been an accountant, help out in your line of expertise.

Face to face

One of my clients, James, took the idea of giving back to a whole new, and personal, level. When he heard that the South African Depression and Anxiety Group (SADAG) needed counsellors, he decided that this was for him. After all, he had led a privileged life and believed that it was time to make a difference in his world. So there he was, in a room full of young people, waiting for his interview in the hope of being accepted for training as a counsellor. He was accepted and the training course was both intense and enlightening, with subjects including depression, bipolar disorder, drug addiction, suicide and abuse. But James was invigorated. Despite his nerves, there was no looking back for him.

This is what he had to say: "I found each caller to be grateful that there was someone on the other end of the line who was prepared to listen to them – and to guide them in a positive direction. After every shift, I leave the office feeling that I have helped someone. I have been with SADAG for over a year and have done 62 four-hour shifts – and I have never once regretted my decision to become a counsellor. My life has been enriched. SADAG has given me the opportunity to talk and work with young people of different cultures, races and religions – and to know that we are all the same in different ways. This involvement has given me a more positive outlook on life as well as a fulfilment that money can't buy. I am also delighted that my sell-by date has not expired!"

3. Relationships

The quality of the people in your life is a reflection of the person you are. Research has shown that people who have fulfilling relationships live longer and happier lives than those who don't. Never downplay the importance of feeling connected. It is not uncommon that when people retire, they don't interact with others as often as they should and, as such, start to feel disconnected and despondent. Feeling a part of something is vital during retirement, so try to make an effort to interact with others and to build a world for yourself that consists of people from different areas of your life.

It has been said that you are never less alone than when you are alone. That is because solitude is not the same as loneliness. To be sure, some of the loneliest individuals in the world are constantly surrounded by people. Being alone can be a very empowering experience. Making space in your life for you is important – and daily solitude should be your starting point if you want to achieve self-understanding and self-acceptance. Once you establish a meaningful relationship with yourself, you are better positioned to build strong, healthy and lasting relationships with others.

"Let us then, be what we are, and speak what we think, and in all things keep ourselves loyal to truth and the sacred professions of friendship."

AMERICAN POET AND EDUCATOR,
HENRY WADSWORTH LONGFELLOW

Whether your working life consisted of working in an office, travelling the world or being a soccer mom, you had built-in daily contact with a variety of people. In retirement you have to make a conscious effort to interact with others. You have to find ways to replace the sense of community that work provided. In retirement, you will probably have less opportunity to interact with former work friends than you did before.

Retirement is your opportunity to make changes. This is when you get to develop a network of meaningful relationships from across all the areas of your life. And, best of all, you'll have the time to enjoy them! Retirement affords you the opportunity to go out there and join a club or society of like-minded people. From bridge clubs, to bird-watching societies, from book clubs to wine-tasting groups, you can be sure that there is an association of people who share your passions. You just need to find them. Your wealth lies in your relationships with others, so make your retirement a rich one by creating a wealth of relationships in your life. Share your life with the people in it.

Face to face

Jean and Paul came to see me as Paul had retired and given up his work six months before. Jean and Paul were finding the transition challenging to say the least, even though they had been excited about it before the time. Jean had not worked since her children were born and had kept herself busy: she was involved with LifeLine; she spent two afternoons a week with her grandchildren; she spent time being creative by doing ceramics and pottery; and walked with friends three mornings a week, with chats and coffee to follow. In Paul's pre-retirement days, he had worked very long hours, not having much extra time for anything other than work – and then needing downtime to recover from work! Despite a wonderful, celebratory road trip across the USA as the ideal initiation into retirement, reality set in once they got back home. Because while Jean's life continued, Paul's still had to start. While Paul didn't expect his wife to be home having lunch with him every day, he also didn't expect to feel as lost and alone as he did.

Paul, you see, had retired *from* something. But he had not worked out what he was retiring *to*. So, we began working together – firstly to work out what he was going to do. And then, with Jean now a part of the discussions, what she could exchange so that they could do a few things together. They shared with me some of what they had learnt during this time of introspection.

Firstly, you are no good to anybody unless you have worked out what you want for yourself. What does this mean? That the first relationship to work on is the one you have with yourself! Secondly, Paul and Jean needed time apart, time to follow their individual dreams. As such, Jean carried on her LifeLine work as well as her hobbies, while Paul started some hobbies of his own, joining a woodworking club and signing up for a writing course – he'd always wanted to write a book – as well as researching his family tree. Thirdly, this couple realised that while it was lovely to come home and share the events of their day over a glass of wine, it was vital that they shared common interests. For Jean and Paul, it was the love of travel. And so Paul took to organising international getaways, making sure to include trips that offered cooking courses, as they had discovered that they both loved cooking different countries' cuisine.

Paul, who had not been a hands-on dad, began to see his grandchildren as the amazing gift that they were, and Jean, who had been more involved than he, helped facilitate her husband's newfound family role. They chose to take my suggestion of having a date night once a week, which is a wonderful way to connect regularly. If you haven't done that yet, you should try it! A fun way to do it is to write down some date ideas, put them into a jar and pull out a new suggestion each week. That way, there's an element of spontaneity and surprise – and a commitment to trying activities and outings you wouldn't normally do.

4. Money

Yes, you may be retiring but that does not mean your money has to stop working for you. The bottom line is that you may be retired for longer than you have worked so why should you only make ultra-conservative investments? Your money *has* to make money for you. And the same principles of compounding interest need to apply. Compounding interest is essential. Einstein called compound interest the eighth Natural Wonder of the World. First prize is for your money to earn *more* money for you – without you having to do much. Allowing investments time to perform will be vitally important in determining how well your money works for you.

What you *are* responsible for, however, is that you spend within the budget that you have allocated for that year. From the conversations I have had with my clients over the years, I have come to understand that this is their number one fear – that their money will not last. It's important that you consult with a financial planner who can, with reasonable accuracy, calculate what age you'll be when your money is expected to start running out. Being armed with this information puts you back in control of what rate of return you need your money to generate, how long you need to carry on earning a salary for and what your monthly spending budget needs to be set at.

"Riches are not an end of life, but an instrument of life."

AMERICAN SPEAKER AND SOCIAL REFORMER,
HENRY WARD BEECHER

This, however, is when emotions are at an all-time high. The unknown feels scary and we know already that retirement is one of the most stressful of life's transitions. It's not uncommon to be fearful of not having enough to get by on, which makes us open to riskier investments. But fear can also result in no decision being made at all – and that's no good either. Fear has caused many retirees to be too scared to spend their money or so fearful of the future that they don't get the financial advice they need. Knowing where you stand is better than not knowing; a head-in-the-sand approach is not a useful one here! You may want your financial position to be better, but you need to work within the parameters you have. Finding a financial planner who specialises in this particular transition would be an absolute asset – literally! You need an objective opinion to make informed, unemotional decisions.

Having a partner help you work out what income you need to generate from your pension/provident fund or what rate of drawdown you need from your living annuity is ideal. Whatever the case, knowing where you stand financially is an essential step towards getting the foundations in place before your money can be invested effectively. It is also important to understand what liquidity is and what it's for. In Chapter 10, we explore this in more detail. Putting a proper financial plan in place that relates to the life you want may take many meetings but each one of them is worth it.

Face to face

Andrew was a 65-year-old client of mine. At the time, his pension fund was valued at R3 million and he had saved R2.5 million in unit trust funds. His lifestyle expenses were R30 000 per month and this needed to be protected against inflation – we assumed 6% inflation – for the rest of his life. We knew that Andrew's financial plan at that time and his chosen investment strategy targeted a return of inflation-plus-4% for the rest of his life and suited his life goals. On examination, however, it became evident that if he continued in his current lifestyle, his investments would run out when he was around 90 years old. Obviously, Andrew wanted to know that the funds would last him right up until he blew out all the candles on his last birthday cake. If that came before the age of 90, fine. But if not, Andrew needed to have other options.

My advice? Andrew needed to either spend less or continue earning an income. He was finding it difficult to spend less as he was already financially stretched, which meant that the only option open to him was to find employment. Part-time work whereby he earned just R10 000 per month for five years would reduce the pressure on his investment assets – so much so that his money would only run out at approximately 94. By this small contribution towards expenses, Andrew would be able to add four years to the time period his money would last. Working for even more years would mean that his savings would last even longer. And so, the smallest adjustments – to either savings or spending – can substantially impact the end result. This is a very simple but empowering example. Acting wisely sooner rather than later is the key. What can we control to help our money last longer? We can spend less, supplement our retirement income by working more and invest our money for optimum returns.

5. Learn

Learning and loving to learn are essential for a balanced retirement. Are you doing enough to keep your mind active? Don't underestimate how easily you can become complacent about learning. You may find that you have to make a conscious effort to challenge yourself daily. Whatever the case, your mental health is vital to your overall wellbeing; it's a case of use it or lose it!

> *"Live as if you were to die tomorrow.*
> *Learn as if you were to live forever."*
>
> Indian civil rights activist, Mohandas K. Gandhi

Retirement is an exciting season. It's when you can go back to your child-like state of being curious about the world around you, of being aware and awestruck about the reality of being alive. Make a decision to be open to learning new things and be committed to curiosity. Why not learn about a new culture or religion? Or enroll to study something that has always interested you. If you have never painted, pick up a paintbrush. If you love crossword puzzles, try Sudoku. Be a mentor to someone; start a conversation with someone. Small gestures towards looking at and learning about life can go a long way towards stimulating your mind. Active mental activity is as crucial to your emotional health as it is to your physical wellbeing.

Face to face

Here is a letter from Lynda Smith, an industry colleague and client. She embraced her second half in an exemplary way and saw this season as a time to learn – and to find her love for life again.

"I sat quietly in my home office thinking about how fast the first 50 years of my life had passed by. The year was 2007 and I was reflecting on the roller-coaster ride I had been on for the past two years. And now, all of a sudden, it seemed quiet and depressing. I remember thoughts going through my mind, including, 'I can die now; I have done the job I was put on this earth to do.' These thoughts were a mixture of many parts of my life's journey, all of which I was experiencing at the same time – probably because I had never really processed everything I had been through in those last few years. There had been a divorce; a business I had been involved in for 15 years had come to an end; both my children had got married and left the country, and a business contract had come to an end. And all this as I turned 50! The picture of what my life would look like beyond this point was blank.

I spent a few months feeling sorry for myself – something most mothers go through after giving their children roots and then having to let them go as they make their way in the world. I loved being a parent and the reality of my empty nest was a blow to my perspective on the future. I then gave myself a little pep talk, realising that I probably had another 25 good years ahead of me and best I pull myself together and look at what I could do with my life! We all have skills, talents and things we are passionate about. I made the decision to take myself on a new adventure to discover what the next part of this journey would look like.

The first thing I did was to move house. I moved from Johannesburg to Hartbeestpoort Dam, into a secure estate where I could make friends and enjoy community – and country life. I was self-employed so it didn't really matter where I lived – as long as I had my computer and connectivity. I am passionate about social change and so, in 2009, I enrolled at GIBS to study Social Entrepreneurship. What a wonderful opportunity to study a subject I'm so passionate about. The journey of discovering what I wanted to do next didn't just pop into my head one day. It was a path that included reading and reflecting; this was a road filled with both joy and pain. I took time to explore what I really wanted to do – as well as look at what the world needed from me. From this process, I emerged the person I am today.

I am a number of years – and four grandchildren – on from that now. It has been a six-year journey on which I re-evaluated each area of my life, slowly putting the pieces of my personal puzzle back together. Finances were a challenge and I am so grateful for the realisation of the importance of an actual financial plan. In turn, I discovered that helping people with their transformations is what I love doing. And today I find myself busier and more fulfilled than I've ever been. I started a business that helps fellow baby boomers to navigate the amazing journey towards retirement and also returned to my long-held passion, that of helping to set up and manage a non-profit business that focuses on early childhood development. I love the fact that I can make a difference, make a living and enjoy life – all at the same time. None of this would be possible without being prepared to learn more about myself and what I still had to contribute to the world."

6. Health

The quality of your life will be affected by the physical limitations your body is subject to. This affects the extent to which you are able to enjoy your retirement. The good news is that your quality of life is completely in your control. So, choose to make good lifestyle choices and aim to make the most *of* – and get the best *from* – your body.

It's all too easy to blame poor health on ageing; being healthy is overwhelmingly in your control. Studies show that only 20% of how we age can be attributed to genes; 50% is determined by our lifestyle choices. This means that the power of your health is in your hands. You have the power to regulate factors such as diet, exercise, pollutants, health habits and smoking. For most people, retirement translates into more time, which means you have more opportunity to focus on your wellbeing. So why not devote a good portion of it to being healthy? Take charge of your health and stay engaged in life. You may not be an enthusiastic gym bunny or want to climb mountains, but choose a form of exercise you enjoy. Find one that resonates with who you are.

CONTRIBUTORS TO OVERALL HEALTH

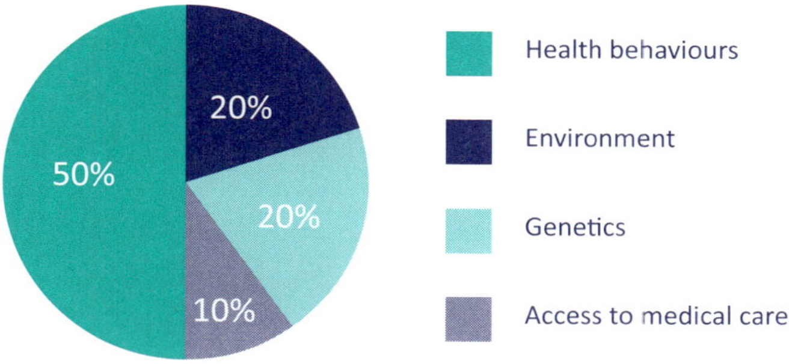

Three lifestyle choices we make daily predict whether we will develop the big four chronic non-communicable diseases that presently kill 60% of the people on the planet.

The three lifestyle choices

1. Smoking
2. Diet
3. Exercise

The big four

1. Cancer
2. Cardiovascular disease
3. Diabetes
4. Chronic lung disease

But health is more than physical health. Emotional health is a key consideration when it comes to your overall health. It has everything to do with your mental attitude, a "spiralling up" or "spiralling down" if you will. If we encourage each other to have "spiralling up" conversations instead of "spiralling down" ones (where perhaps we're compelled to tell an even more horrific story than our friend or sympathise too much so that you both feel worse off after talking with each other), we'll be much better off for it. Practise gratitude to ward off grumpiness. Some say that statistically, we'll live seven-and-a-half years longer with a positive attitude. I'm not sure about that but we have nothing to lose by giving it a try, right? To my mind, attitude is the mind's paintbrush: it colours every aspect of life.

Face to face

One of my clients, Anthony, was extremely despondent about the idea of retirement. To his mind, South Africa, the country he lived in – and loved – was falling apart. He couldn't sleep at night and his health was at an all-time low. When we looked at his 168 hours a week, we noted that he was listening to the news every hour, on the hour! This in itself was causing him great stress – even if the news reflected accurately some of what was going on around him. By the time Anthony got into bed each night, he was too despondent to rest. So, I suggested not listening to the news! This may sound like ostrich-head-in-the-sand advice but what Anthony needed to do – and what he did – was shift his worldview. His listening to the news was not making a difference to what was happening in the country. But it was making a difference to him. And so he took my advice.

Moreover, he joined an organisation focused on making a difference in society. This commitment meant that he was in a position to make a positive impact on the world instead of spreading more doom and gloom in it. Today, Anthony is a different person, using his energy positively – and for the good of others and, ultimately, himself.

7. Purpose

It may sound a little idealistic to you – the idea of a having a "purpose". But in truth, real fulfilment comes from living a life where you have some sense that there is something that you are *meant* to be – or do. You may not have found that thing that you were truly "meant" for yet but it's never too late to initiate the process of personal growth and, ultimately, purpose. In fact, they go hand in hand; the one is integral to the other. You can't discover your purpose if you don't know yourself. In retirement, you're equipped with life experience *and* time. And so you can do both. You *do* need to believe, however, that you have a purpose. Believing that you have a purpose makes for a much richer life tapestry ... even before you uncover it. So, spend some time thinking about what really makes you happy, what it might be that makes you tick. And then pursue a life that incorporates those things. Yearn to be better than you are. Be open to growing. And pursue your passions.

It is often during the transition to retirement that people take the time and energy to search for something deeper – for something to bring more meaning to their lives. Looking inward, inside yourself, is the best way to find this meaning. You need to be looking for signs of the true "you". Seek out activities that make you feel alive inside, that evoke feelings of passion and peace. And, if you can't come up with anything meaningful, be open to exploring the possibilities. We often spend our lives searching for answers that we already have. Finding your purpose has everything to do with who you are innately, already. Follow your joy; a life without purpose can lead to a disassociation from life – and from yourself. A life with purpose, on the other hand, can lead to an incredible love of life itself.

Face to face

This Face to face is a personal one. That's because it's mine. Well, it's mine in the sense that it includes some input from someone close to my heart. What it does is get to the core of some invigorating input by inspirational author and motivational speaker, Colleen-Joy Page, the person close to my heart. Her words have impacted my life in ways that are now immeasurable, as I've gone within myself to explore my own purpose in life. As you pore over this section, I wish the same for you. So take a moment to slow down, to consider Colleen-Joy's perspective – and then your own – on this thing called life.

Colleen-Joy has the strong sense that "most of us believe that our life purpose is about doing something – that we would add the most meaning to our lives through our actions. As a result, we regularly face painful questions like: 'Am I doing the right thing?', 'Am I doing enough?', 'Am I doing it well enough?', 'What if I am putting all this effort into doing something that is not my real purpose?' and 'What if I do all of this and still feel unfulfilled?'" Do you relate? Do you sometimes feel that your day is filled with doing – and yet you still feel unfulfilled? Colleen-Joy's view is that this is because your life purpose is not about *doing*. It's about *being*. "Doing is significant; it has a place," she says. "But it needs to be second place to being."

I've been challenged by her contention that our life purpose is to be our truest self. And that living our life purpose brings the ultimate fulfilment. For her, "Fulfilment comes through the experience of being your truest self freely in the world. If your focus is on doing, you will miss the point. You'll miss out on the adventure of unfolding who you are in the world. You'll also risk putting time and energy into paths that don't reflect who you are; paths that lead to a life that feels empty and unfulfilling."

Doing things that are empty of who you really are is frustrating. She asks: "Have you lost touch with the part of you that feels alive and free?

Do you feel like you are hiding part or all of yourself? Do you feel like something is missing from your life, but you are not entirely sure what it is? If it feels like something is missing, it is very likely true that what is missing is the true 'you'." Do you know that your life has everything to do with being you – and not anyone else? Don't do what other people do – even though, says Colleen-Joy, "the real you may be buried deep within yourself or afraid to stand tall in your life. Your life's purpose is to fully be in this world and say lovingly in your heart, 'I am this'. It may sound like a simple thing, but the quest to unveil and be your true self in the world is the greatest of life quests. And the rewards of the quest are to find the greatest treasures life has to offer."

So, what is your purpose? Who are you? It is important to bring who you *are* to what you *do* – and the world at large.

8. Play

Being able to play and have fun will make you feel alive and euphoric. But you need to identify the activities that bring you that level of satisfaction. The good news is that retirement gives you the freedom to discover what brings you immense pleasure. Once you know that, you can consciously and actively include those things in your life.

> *"And in the end, it's not the years in your life that count. It's the life in your years."*
>
> AMERICAN PRESIDENT, ABRAHAM LINCOLN

Having fun is the most natural human experience. You're happiest when you're having fun. That's just the way the world works. When you play, you experience a childlike freedom that fuels your enthusiasm for life. And the truth is that much learning takes place when you are truly enjoying yourself. Please believe that it is *never* too late to engage in an activity that bring you happiness – be it a hobby or a passion.

Travel is one of the great pleasures of life, is it not? Many retired people try to incorporate travel into their worlds. Travel doesn't have to be purely for leisure: it can inspire, fulfil, educate. Best of all, your travel routine doesn't have to be cast in stone; it can vary from year to year. One year could see you studying famous artworks; another could see you visiting the great architectural marvels of the world. Whether you travel locally or internationally – in five-star luxury or on a shoe-string budget – travel is a wonderful way to enhance your retirement experience. You can make your retirement the grandest of all life's adventures!

Face to face

Clients David and Liz undertook a bucket list trip, one that should inspire all of us to make our dreams come true. Liz, at age 67, had never visited Namibia and Botswana before. Little did she know that David, just shy of 80, wasn't daunted by the prospect of wading through a river in a Land Rover – or being sniffed at, at close range, by a curious elephant! And this is exactly what happened on their safari of a lifetime. This intrepid couple motored over vast distances, through remote areas and in deep sand tracks to get to the r destinations – often places of such beauty and wildness that it took their breath away. Not only did they undertake this demanding trip on their own, but they camped in far-flung game reserves with the only light around them the flicker of the African stars.

David and Liz attribute the success of their trip to being fully equipped and prepared – and to being sufficiently mentally and physical fit to undertake a journey of such magnitude. For each of us, the challenge is to have similar courage and conviction to undertake whatever road trip of life calls us.

Have you been inspired by some of the stories in this chapter? I hope so. Not too long ago, Jason, one of my clients, phoned me and said to me: "Kim, you know all that advice you keep giving me? Well. It's working. I've taken up guitar lessons – at 74 – and I'm travelling to Paris next year to do a cooking course! My golf may not be getting better; but I can tell you something, Kim, it's not getting worse!" Jason has a point, doesn't he? There is a lot to be said for being creative about the new possibilities ahead of us. Are you starting to get excited at the idea of these eight elements – work, giving back, relationships, money, learning, health, purpose and play – co-existing in exciting juxtaposition with one other? If so, then bring on the balance.

A Bucket Wheel is an invaluable tool for accurately identifying what is truly important to you.

CHAPTER 9

A Bucket Wheel with Balance

"Life is like an ever-shifting kaleidoscope – a slight change, and all patterns alter."

Real Happiness, Sharon Salzberg

In many ways, this chapter is a culmination of your journey to date, a destination of sorts. Here is where change brings the altering of patterns, the dreaming of new dreams. This has been happening to you from the inside out – in such a way that your retirement plan starts to take shape. Your ideas have been flowing; you have been asking questions of yourself. Your patterns have been altering and you have been getting the answers you've been looking for.

BUCKET WHEEL

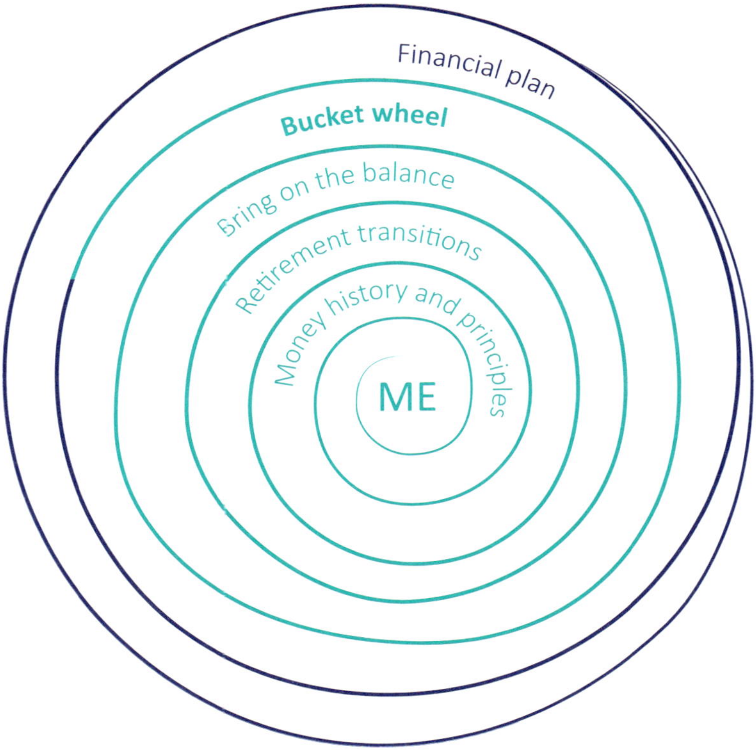

I can't emphasise enough how important it is to distance yourself from how other people approach retirement. Your retirement has everything to do with *you* and what resonates with *you*; it's about *your* dreams. This journey, as you would have come to realise by now as you worked through each of the Retiremeant Reflections so far, is an individual one. There is no one right route – and no one right destination. And we should respect ourselves enough to allow our individuality to shine through. We have shared many ideas, haven't we, as we have worked through the life-planning meeting that this book represents. Now it is time for those ideas to translate into some specifics.

A list for life

You probably know the origin of the words "bucket list". Yes, it's a list of the goals you want to achieve before you, you know, "kick the bucket". And it's an essential element of your retirement plan; it's the place, in effect, to where your retirement plan leads you to. The objective of creating a bucket list is not to create some kind of race against time. The point of a bucket list is to maximise every moment we have and to inspire us to live life to the full. Your bucket list is a reminder to you of all the things you still want to achieve in your time on earth – so that instead of wasting your time on meaningless activities, you direct your energy towards what matters most. It is the practical preparation that lays the foundation for that Disney magic we looked at in Chapter 3 to come true.

It is important that you set aside considerable time and focus your energy properly when it comes to creating your bucket list. It has to be an accurate reflection of your dreams and ambitions. A well-thought-out bucket list is an invaluable tool for accurately identifying what is truly important to you. Then you and your financial planner can tailor-make a financial plan to support your lifelong dreams. Your bucket list is the best indicator of what money you will need and how your money needs to work for you. Most people allow how much money they have to dictate the type of life they live in retirement. But after reading this book, you will not be one of those people. You have put money in its proper place. You are master over your money.

"I long to accomplish a great and noble task, but it is my chief duty to accomplish small tasks as if they were great and noble."

American author and political activist, Helen Keller

From buckets to balance

Okay, so you've noticed that this book looks at retirement a little differently from most books. So why would it not be the same for bucket lists? While the traditional idea of a bucket list is extremely helpful in that it focuses you on tangible objectives you want to meet, it generally conjures up ideas of things to *do*. What *Retiremeant* has been proposing – from the very first Retiremeant Reflection you did – relates not only to what you *do* but who you *are*. Please let me introduce then: the Bucket *Wheel*®.

I imagine that you would have found the chapters on balance an innovative way to see your world. Maybe you thought about things a little differently, seeing the value in investing in areas you might otherwise not have looked at. Well, what I'd like to do now is integrate that idea of balance with your bucket list to bring you your Bucket Wheel. Your Bucket Wheel is a holistic approach to the culmination of your journey to date and it reflects all of the eight elements as areas for you to see dreams come to pass in. Bucket lists that consist only of a string of international travel destinations might be ticked off one by one. But unless your bucket list is effected in all of the areas as shown in the image that follows, you will find yourself less fulfilled than you thought.

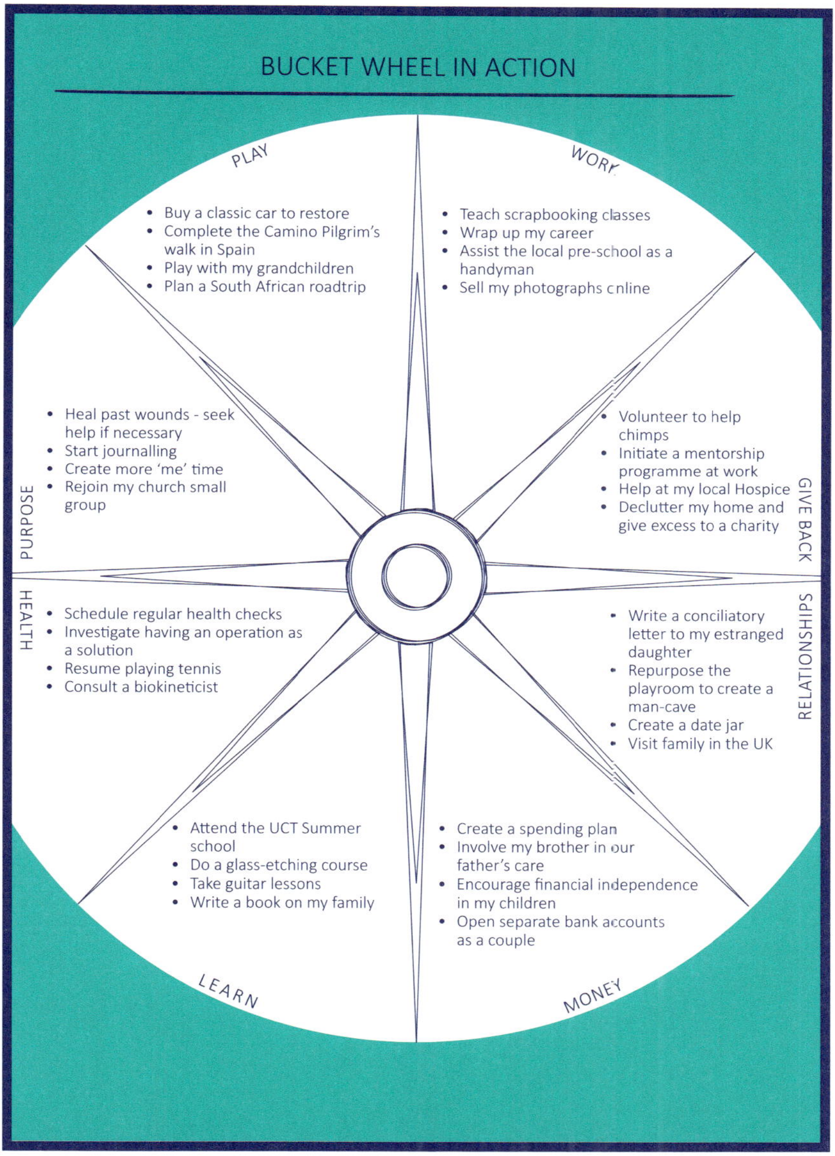
BUCKET WHEEL IN ACTION
PLAY
Buy a classic car to restore
Complete the Camino Pilgrim's walk in Spain
Play with my grandchildren
Plan a South African roadtrip
WORK
Teach scrapbooking classes
Wrap up my career
Assist the local pre-school as a handyman
Sell my photographs online
GIVE BACK
Volunteer to help chimps
Initiate a mentorship programme at work
Help at my local Hospice
Declutter my home and give excess to a charity
RELATIONSHIPS
Write a conciliatory letter to my estranged daughter
Repurpose the playroom to create a man-cave
Create a date jar
Visit family in the UK
MONEY
Create a spending plan
Involve my brother in our father's care
Encourage financial independence in my children
Open separate bank accounts as a couple
LEARN
Attend the UCT Summer school
Do a glass-etching course
Take guitar lessons
Write a book on my family
HEALTH
Schedule regular health checks
Investigate having an operation as a solution
Resume playing tennis
Consult a biokineticist
PURPOSE
Heal past wounds - seek help if necessary
Start journalling
Create more 'me' time
Rejoin my church small group

Face to face

Joanne came to see me some time ago. She was retired, but unhappily so. This life phase was a disappointment to her – so much so that she was missing working at the advertising agency that she had owned. She could not get her head around the idea of a bucket list as she didn't think she had enough money for much dreaming of any kind. And besides, she felt weighed down by responsibilities: she was looking after her grandchildren every day and even though she loved being with them, the image she had had of retirement – of painting and travelling – and her reality of looking after three children as a support to her daughter, who needed to work fulltime, were worlds apart.

Joanne had come to see what return we could secure for her retirement investments. Her income was coming from dividends from her share portfolio, but Joanne wasn't sure what she and her husband could realistically live on based on these investments and as such, they lived conservatively. Their money memories had been shaped by their respective parents' wartime experiences – and their own childhoods of relative poverty. And yet, on closer examination, I noted that Joanne – and her husband, Jack – had built a very successful business. This had translated into sizeable investments – so sizeable in fact, that Joanne and Jack's money was only going to run out when they reached age 155!

This meant that not only was their daughter going to inherit a sizeable amount of money but that they themselves were better positioned, financially, than they thought they were. And yet none of this counted for much because neither Joanne nor Jack – or Kelly, their daughter – had spent much time exploring their relationships with money or creating a Bucket Wheel. Instead, all three of them were head-down in the details of their lives. Joanne's daughter Kelly was working as a vet – a job she didn't like – when she was desperate to be a more involved mom. Her kids, in turn, were being raised by Joanne and an au pair – all this when

Kelly's dream was to be a teacher, so much did she love children. Kelly's hope was to teach at her children's school. So I had a client who was disappointed by retirement with a daughter who was miserable.

But the power of the process – and its resulting Bucket Wheel – were just around the corner for them. As I do with all my clients, I looked at their money memories and we explored their history with, and relationship to, money. Once we did that, they realised that their fear of not having enough money was not based on reality but in a perception created by the past. Plus, they had been so overly cautious around spending that they were dooming their daughter to an impressive inheritance – along with the inability to ever enjoy it! She too would have to change how she saw money in order to put it to best use. After doing some Disney dreaming together, we were able to identify many unfulfilled dreams. So much of their lives had been focused on growing the business of their advertising agency that their dreams had been left to die.

So, we started to toy with a few ideas. What if we shuffled things around a little? What about allowing their daughter to access some of her inheritance upfront – instead of her waiting twenty years until her children had left home and she had missed the chance to spend more time with them? Yes, it would mean that her daughter would inherit less money. But they were going to share in fulfilling each other's dreams now, which in truth was much more exciting. The daughter was going to go back to university for her teaching qualification, while at the same time being able to spend more time with her children. Of the eight areas, Kelly's shift took into authentic account those of Money, Work, Relationships and Learn on her Bucket Wheel. How exciting! And a happier Kelly meant that she was better positioned to tap into her Play too!

Joanne and Jack would no longer be required to collect kids, manage homework and attend the various sports matches. This meant that their Bucket Wheel could be looked at more earnestly too. Once they gave themselves the time and space to envision, it emerged that it wasn't just their daughter who had a dream. They did too; by looking at the area of Money with new eyes, they were able to transform their areas of Learn and Play. Joanne wanted to do a writing course, go for piano lessons and attend more art classes, while her husband wanted to play golf and travel overseas with Joanne, Kelly and the grandchildren. Which is exactly what he started to do. Joanne, Jack – and Kelly and her family – are all the happier for taking their Bucket Wheels seriously, the area most positively impacted being that of Relationships, of course!

Watching the wheel

Now it's your turn. You're going to take some time to look over your answers from Retiremeant Reflections 13 and 14 and, from those, start compiling your very own Bucket Wheel. You're going to reflect on how balanced you feel and assess what is working – and what isn't. These are the beginnings of creating our own Bucket Wheel. This will reflect the things you would still like to *do* – and *be* – in your life ahead. As you feel you've accomplished something on your Bucket Wheel, revisit it, slotting in new goals as you go. Your Bucket Wheel will help you focus on what's important to you in your second half while at the same time ensuring that you are mindful of all eight areas.

The objective of compiling a bucket wheel is not to create a race against time or to instil fear. The point is to maximise every moment of our existence and to inspire us to live our lives to the fullest. It's a reminder of all the things we want to achieve in our time on earth, so that instead of wasting our time on activities that don't fulfil us, we direct our energy to what matters most to us.

Before you get started though, take note of these guidelines.

Nine Bucket Wheel Nos

Here are some recommendations to help you put your Bucket Wheel together and maintain it, as we direct our energy towards what matters most to us.

1. **Don't write it all at once.** This isn't an easy list to write. You may get to five or ten things and then hit a blank. Don't get discouraged: just take some time off before you come back to it. This is an ongoing process. Many people don't complete their wheels because they are continually adding to them. Think of it as a working document; whenever you think of something, write it down and add to it.
2. **Don't try to be somebody else.** The world is a vastly interesting place. Think of your unique interests and work on a few ideas that set you apart from everyone else. Just be yourself.
3. **Don't wander from the wheel.** Make sure you spend time on all eight areas of your Bucket Wheel: learn, be mindful of money matters, work on your relationships, find your personal purpose, make sure you give back, don't neglect your work, don't ignore your health and remember to play!
4. **Don't go solo.** You might know exactly what you want on your Bucket Wheel. But there might be things you've never considered before. So read other people's lists. Allow yourself to be inspired by people around you. You're not going to be copying everyone's ideas but you can get the juices flowing by sharing in other people's excitement.

5. **Don't make it impossible.** Yes, it's great to dream big. But make some dreams easier to achieve than others. If all of your goals are difficult to accomplish – if they're all expensive, unrealistic and time-consuming – your list isn't going to be very effective. You'll be setting yourself up for failure and you'll find yourself discouraged. Making a decision to take a weekend away somewhere special can be as wonderful an experience as that round-the-world cruise.
6. **Don't make it too far off.** It's always good to have long-term goals to work towards. But make sure you include something that you can do *today*. In order for this to be successful, you need to get rid of the "someday" mindset. Life is short so you had better get started. There are things you can do right now that you've always wanted to but have been putting off. Well, now is that time.
7. **Don't be vague.** Set goals. Your Bucket Wheel can only be effective if it is accompanied by clear goals, a timeline and a plan of action. These goals must be specific and realistic. It's also a good idea to earmark specific items that you want to achieve each year. This is a good way to keep the momentum going.
8. **Don't be dull.** Have fun! Creating a Bucket Wheel should feel like having fun. It is all about taking steps towards doing what you want with your life. Don't let stress – or what you think you *should* be including – creep in. This is about *your* life. Everyone is going to use their list differently. So, if you are finding it hard to accomplish a particular goal, work on something else and go back to it later. You have plenty of time – more years in retirement than we initially thought, remember?

9. **Don't stick it in a drawer.** Keep your Bucket Wheel accessible to you. Put it up somewhere where you – and even your loved ones – can see it. This way, you can be inspired by all the good times that are ahead.

RETIREMEANT REFLECTION **16** Bring on the Bucket Wheel

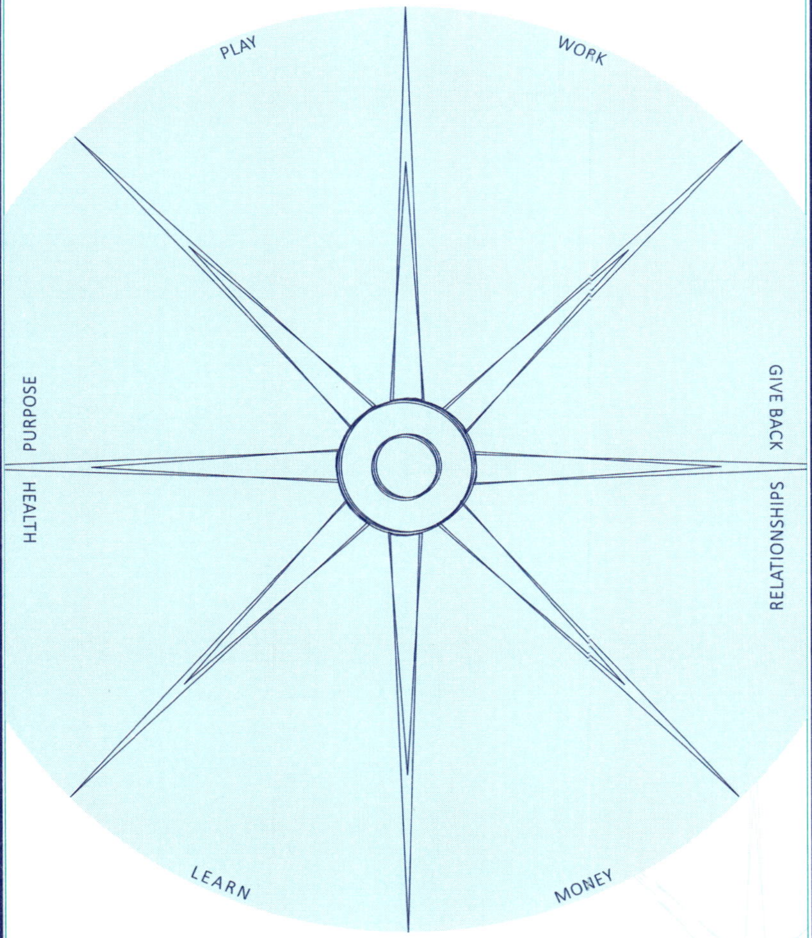

Download a free template of this Retiremeant Reflection by visiting www.retiremeant.co.za

The message of this book has been to preserve and enhance the greatest asset you have – *you*. We can't choose how many years we live. But we *can* choose how much life these years will bring us. Change in life brings uncertainty but our ability to overcome will be determined by our attitude. So make the choice to actively participate in creating your best future. Retirement gives you the freedom to achieve unfulfilled dreams and goals – on your own terms and in your own time. So bring your "A" game to your retirement and make each day count, starting today.

A holistic life plan and accurate financial plan: worth so much more when combined to make money and meaning meet – that is RetiremeAnt!

CHAPTER 10

Making your Money Work in Retirement

"He is rich or poor according to what he is, not what he has."

American speaker and social reformer, Henry Ward Beecher

FINANCIAL PLAN

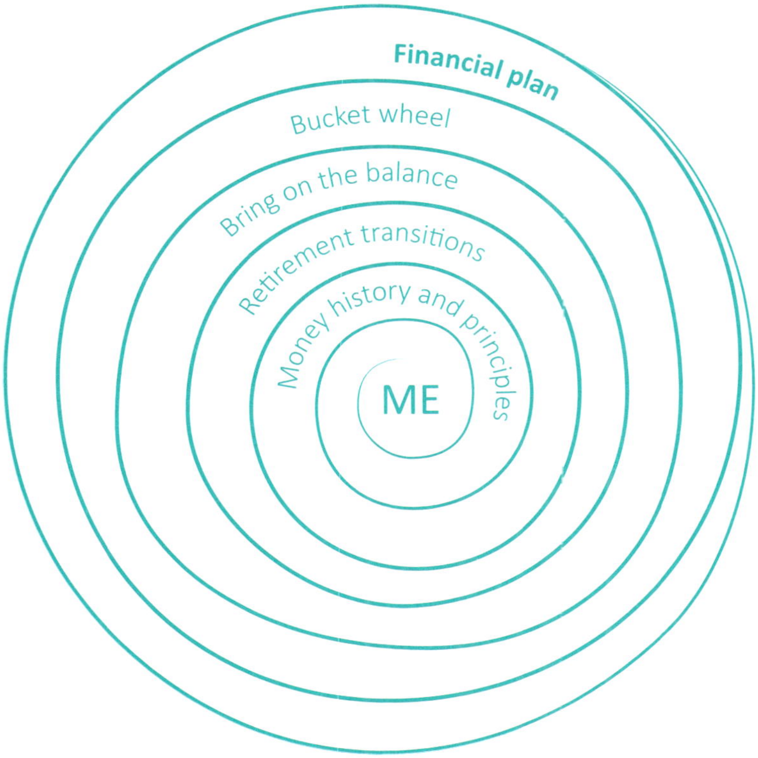

When we started this book, our premise was that your money needed to work for you. And nothing has changed. In the conversations that we've shared through the chapters that comprise this book, we have focused on various areas of your life. We've covered everything from your first money memory to your personality, your spouse's personality and how you can see the world from his or her perspective, from examining your career and exploring your thoughts on retirement to how to bring balance to your world – *and* to your Bucket Wheel! All of this work (work I am sure benefitted you) was for one purpose and one purpose only: to enable you to get the most out of your retirement. So much so, in fact, that the word *retirement* became ***retire****meant* in an attempt to inject as much meaning and mindfulness as possible into this second half of your life.

But, to do that – to get the most out of your retirement – we have to take two more significant steps, which means that this chapter is crucial. Remember our Disney dreaming in Chapter 3? Do you remember that we referred to four steps? They were: vision, planning, critic and action, and in Retiremeant Reflection 3 we took some time to dream and plan, leaving the critic (that part of your thinking that takes the practical into account) and action elements of the exercise aside for a moment. The purpose of that exercise was to allow you to dream without being short-circuited by pragmatic considerations or objections based on reality.

Well, here is where we draw our attention to the critic and action aspects of dreaming the Disney way. Yes, we are going to let the critic back into the proverbial room. And then, from the place of that reality check, create an action plan for an A-Game retirement.

Come in, critic

As much as this book has been about your empowerment, about your coming to terms with who you are, what you believe and what you want, it is also about the powerful role that reality plays in making those dreams come true. There is a lot to be learnt from the most powerful person in your life – you. And from those in the know, which we'll get to in a minute. But let's start with you.

RETIREMEANT REFLECTION 17 What is the Critic saying?

Take a look back at your answers to Retiremeant Reflection 3 in Chapter 3. Remember the vision and planning notes you made? Well, it's time to get pen in hand and put the critic to work. Here is where you allow your perceived reality back into your headspace, where you get to entertain all those reasons that your dream could never come true. This is not to hinder the process but to enhance it. If your dream is going to come true, it has to be able to stand up to reality, right? So, in this exercise, we get to embrace the naysayer. As you do this exercise, allow the proverbial critic to come up with only one objection at a time though and then work on a solution immediately, with a positive, planning attitude until all objections have been worked through.

The Disney Way refers to this next step as the "sweat box" stage. In this stage, you are finding objections to work with. Once you have thoroughly gone through the three Disney steps, having given yourself the freedom to go back to the vision stage at any point if necessary, you can consolidate and finish with a good Step 3. This exercise can take 30 minutes or an hour – or even an entire day. Here we go.

How would your retirement look if it turned out well? Briefly refer again to the dreams this picture is composed of.

....

....

....

....

....

What could go wrong in trying to realise this dream? What are the biggest obstacles you think you face?

....

....

....

....

....

....

How do you think you could prevent or address that? How could you overcome these obstacles?

....

....

....

....

....

....

RETIREMEANT REFLECTION 17 What is the Critic saying?

Name one possible objection to the dream or goal from someone you know. What would it be?

....

....

....

....

....

....

Pen a response to that person here, pointing out why you believe your dream could, in fact, come true.

....

....

....

....

....

....

What needs to be in place for you to realise your dream?

....

....

....

....

....

....

Download a free template of this Retiremeant Reflection by visiting www.retiremeant.co.za

Allowing this "critical" thinker into your space to ask practical questions allows for an empowering shift. And now we take things one step further by allowing yet *another* critic into our dreaming space – money itself. If there is not enough money, some dreams have to be adapted. As much as this book is about empowering you to get to grips with you and your money, it is also very much about really and truly making those dreams come true. That means that you need to have a sense of where to go from here – and who to talk to. This is where the financial life planner hears all your dreams and works out a plan to get your money to support your dreams and plans for retirement.

There are many skilled financial planning professionals who are equipped to advise you with integrity and intelligence. A financial planner who is positioned to partner with you near, and in, retirement can bring you into one of the most important relationships you will have in your life. Should you opt to go this route and seek professional advice, it is crucial to find someone with whom you feel comfortable, someone with whom you resonate, someone who truly wants to help you reach your goals.

A good financial planner can assist you in the following ways:

- Through a life-planning meeting, your planner can help you determine your goals by encouraging you to explore what it is that you want. Ideally, he or she will ask the right questions about your history and relationship with money so you can put money in its right place – an enabler for the life you want.
- Your planner is positioned to, and will, provide the tools and expertise you need to help create a connection between those goals and your financial resources. Your planner can be someone who ensures that you are getting a Return on Life in addition to a Return on Investment. Someone who knows you well and can challenge you to live the best life you can.
- Your financial planner will offer you objective advice and bring his or her perspective to bear. This is an important consideration at a time when emotions – especially fear and greed – can affect your decisions on how to invest your money.
- Your planner will add the dimension of discipline to your

investment approach. Time in the market is important, and rash decisions could cost you in the long term. Your financial planner will help hone your thinking at critical times.

- Your planner will be able to advise on legislation changes and the impact of these on your investments; someone to walk with you through your life transitions and assess the impact of these transitions on your financial affairs.
- Working with your planner offers you a holistic view, not only of investments but matters relating to tax, liquidity, estate planning, will planning, cash flow planning and risk management.

You may not have considered consulting with a financial planner up until now but he or she may be exactly what you need. If you decide that you do, here are a few tips on what might be best to look for:

- The industry's recommended technical qualification is a Certified Financial Planner (CFP®). Opting to consult with a CFP® will ensure that he or she is armed with the most up-to-date knowledge. The industry requires that CFP®s remain accredited and must therefore remain up-to-date with planning knowledge. The benefit of this goes directly to you, as a client.
- Choose a financial planning specialist who deals in retirement and who will go out of his or her way to understand the specifics of your transition.
- Make sure you choose someone who cares enough to know what you want – and helps find the strategies and solutions that you need. In your mind, it should be someone you could

comfortably give the role of Chief Financial Officer of your life to. This is a person who should be able to help you with every major financial decision that you make. Your future will be shaped by the type of assistance he or she gives, so do your research, choose wisely and trust your gut.

- Find out how your planner will earn his or her fees. This is important. It's ideal, although not always possible, to recruit a planner who charges a fee for a financial plan rather than a fee that is directly relational to a particular set of products. At the very least, your planner should disclose how he will be earning an ongoing fee. This enables you to be aware of any product bias the planner may be affected by and to make informed choices with that in mind.
- It is advisable to find a planner who is as independent as possible and not working for, or affiliated to, a particular financial company to which he or she is obliged to give the investment. Independence means that advice given to you will be as objective as possible.
- Opt for a planner who has a business succession plan in place. You may respect the advice of your particular planner but ensure you know what would happen with your portfolio in the event of something happening to him or her. Would there be someone to take over if this should happen? Be certain you know the answer to this.

Consulting with a financial planner is really the ideal scenario. However, whether you opt for one or not, I want you to be as equipped as you can be in the time leading up to, and during, your second half. While the specifics of your needs and circumstances must be taken into account when it comes to the detail of compiling your financial plan, there are some rules for general application when it comes to creating the best financial plan for you.

See these tips that follow as the fourth step in our Disney process. From here on out, it is all about action – the action of making your dreams a reality by implementing your plan. This point is where your life plan meets your financial plan and has been custom made by you – and hopefully honed by someone in the financial life-planning know you will be set for a truly rewarding and enriching retirement.

FOURTEEN ACTION ITEMS FOR AN A-GAME RETIREMENT FOR YOUR MONEY

Action item 1: Plan for a prolonged retirement

Longevity has increased dramatically in the last hundred years. This means that retirements can easily last 25 or 30 years, with years in retirement outlasting years working in many cases. Generally, people underestimate how many years they will live for and so invariably fail to have enough money saved.

When you do take a more protracted age into account, make sure you consider the ages of both you *and* your spouse. Although we think that our costs will reduce dramatically if there is only one person to be taken care of, this is not the case. Costs for one person in retirement could be as high as 75% of the total cost estimated for two people. My recommendation is that you plan for a lifespan of at least 100 years for the surviving spouse. This way, you also create a buffer for unexpected costs that may arise or market corrections that may need to be factored in.

Action item 2: Involve your partner

As you embark on and plan for this transition, it is imperative that you involve your spouse. I cannot emphasise this enough. When you and your spouse are both engaged in the process of information-sharing and decision-making, you set yourself up for success. My experience has shown that if one partner is not involved, he or she doesn't really buy into what you are trying to achieve and, even unwittingly, can sabotage the process. Even more concerning, in the case of one partner predeceasing the other, if the remaining party has been the disinterested spouse or the spouse had not been included, he or she will have little sense of the financial plan at hand. With just a little bit of the wrong advice, made that much worse by the emotional turmoil that comes with loss and grieving, that person could make a bad investment call, standing to lose much of what the other spouse spent decades building.

It is wise for each spouse to have money invested in his or her own name for the purposes of tax efficiency. Not only is this emotionally empowering but, practically, it ensures that in the event of something happening to one spouse – along with the subsequent freezing of bank accounts – the remaining spouse still has access to money. This means they will have one less thing to worry about at a probably terribly traumatic time.

Action item 3: Know how much you need

Do you have any sense of how much money you need to last you through retirement? You need to. A person's number one fear is running out of money and becoming dependent on others or destitute. So, where do you start? Start at the planning stage. How much do you have? How much do you need? Be realistic regarding what you have, and about the assets you have that can provide you with an income.

Draw up a spending plan or a budget of your monthly expenses – you are welcome to use our useful Spending Plan on page 156 (or download it from www.retiremeant.co.za). Spend the time you need to in order to compile it as accurately as possible for a realistic sense of where things are at. Understanding your spending sheet is crucial to the devising of a good financial plan – and to ensuring that you don't run out of money. When your planner looks at your spending plan, he would look at two aspects: firstly, your normal, monthly living expenses, and secondly, lump sum amounts related to items such as holidays, the buying of a new car, a wedding or renovations for your home. He would then calculate where these monies should be drawn from (annuity/pension or discretionary monies). It is important to always keep in mind that they should be drawn tax effectively (your annuity is taxable), but at the same time protecting your discretionary investments (more liquid investments) to ensure that you have the flexibility to withdraw lump sums when you need them.

With all this information – along with the right financial planning tools – your financial planner can, with a fair degree of accuracy, give you a sense of how long your money will last. To do this, he or she would need to know three things:

1. The current size of your retirement assets, which includes all your savings and investments you have earmarked to fund your retirement.
2. The income you would like to receive on a monthly basis, and any lump-sum drawings you would like to make for special events (children's weddings, overseas holidays) or to fund the items on your "bucket list" (things you would like to do before you die).
3. A rate of investment return or growth that your monies need to grow by, over time. We always look at an amount above inflation, be this, say, 2%, 4% or 6% above inflation. This information is put into a financial planning tool that calculates the age at which your money is most likely to run out.

It is important to note here that the information that emerges from this exercise is only as accurate as the data you input … so don't overestimate your income, or underestimate your expenses – being as realistic as possible is really empowering.

RETIREMEANT REFLECTION 18 Monthly spending sheet

Income	Current	In retirement	Remarks
Salary (You)			
Salary (Your Spouse)			
Rental Income			
Other Investment Income i.e. Dividends/Interest			
Self-employed business profit			
Maintenance			
Other Income i.e. Pension			
TOTAL income per month			
TOTAL income per annum			

Please fill out expenses on page 2

TOTAL expenses per month		
TOTAL expenses per annum		
Monthly Surplus/Defecit		

RETIREMEANT REFLECTION 18 Monthly spending sheet

Income	Current	In retirement	Remarks
Bond repayments			
Rent payable			
Rates and taxes			
Levies			
Electricity			
Telephone			
Cellphone			
Internet			
Clothing			
Groceries / Toiletries, etc.			
Out-of-pocket medical expenses			
Domestic help			
Gardening costs			
Petrol and oil			
Motor vehicle maintenance			
Educational expenses			
Other loan repayments			
Leasing or hire purchase costs			
Health insurance			
Property and contents insurance			
Motor vehicle insurance			
Life insurance / Retirement annuities			
Professional subscriptions			
Entertainment / Alcohol / Tobacco			
Newspapers and magazines			
Social club subscriptions			
Holidays (local only)			
DSTV / MNet			
Pocket money			
Security			
Veterinary expenses			
Miscellaneous			
TOTAL per month			
TOTAL per annum			

Download a free template of this Retiremeant Reflection by visiting www.retiremeant.co.za

Action item 4: Deal with your debt

It is essential to prioritise paying off your debt. Try to pay off your bond before retirement. This helps to reduce your monthly expenditure in your retirement years because, simply put, debt is expensive. Returns from investments taking tax into account are often less than interest being charged on debt, so paying off that debt before retirement will help with cash flow.

Action item 5: Be ready for the risks

To give you optimum peace of mind, make sure that you have a proper sense of some of the risks that retirement may bring. It's not about being afraid – just aware. When devising your financial plan, your planner needs to be looking at what risks you are exposed to or anything that can threaten your financial stability in retirement.

Here are some risks to be aware of:

- Retirement might imply not receiving a salary any more. What is the risk to you of being without this income on a monthly basis?
- Be aware of the risks associated with debt. If you do have debt, what are the risks to which you are exposed should something happen to you unexpectedly? The general rule is: if you can afford to retire, you don't need life insurance. But if you have debt going into retirement, life insurance may be needed.
- There are risks that come with investments – the risk of R100 being worth, say, R95 at the end of any one particular year, for example. Since investment strategies carry risk, make sure that you and your partner have discussed what the best and worst scenarios are. Consider what the risks are if you don't achieve a certain investment return. Being in cash, for example, is a risk: it is recklessly conservative and will not keep up with inflation. Keeping cash is a guaranteed way of saving yourself poor.

- The markets can pose risks. Be aware of the possible risks here as well as the impact of increasing inflation on your financial affairs.
- You might live in a country where you need to consider political risk. Having offshore *and* local investments is recommended.
- Death may expose the surviving spouse to risk. What are the risks associated with you or your spouse dying? Be sure of the implication for the surviving spouse. A spouse who is ignorant of the family's investments may be vulnerable to unscrupulous people who offer seemingly simple solutions.
- Staying abreast of constantly changing legislation is a challenge for the layman – the skill of a professional is essential in this regard.

Action item 6: Stay away from the scams!

No one sets out to lose his or her money. But if a potential investment sounds too good to be true, it probably is! Work on a return on investment that you are comfortable with – one that leaves you able to eat and sleep well at night. Aiming for unrealistic returns causes stress – and the stress and pressure alone can see you lose before you know it.

Your principles should be similar to those of Warren Buffet. For him, a sound investment approach comes down to investing in a diverse range of quality investments at prices that represent good value, with a view to investing for sufficient time, thereby bringing you the returns you planned for.

Action item 7: Keep cash for a crisis

Always keep three months' income in a liquid investment – such as a money market account – so that you are ready to deal with emergencies without having to draw out of your investments. With regard to living annuities, you can only change the level of income drawn once a year at the anniversary date. Your living annuity should not be relied on to cover emergencies but rather to cover your monthly income requirements. Having a liquid investment for unforeseen expenses is vital.

Action item 8: Be mindful of medical matters

Having a medical aid in retirement is non-negotiable and it's essential, from a costing perspective, that you assume a higher inflation rate for medical expenses. Medical costs escalate, partly because you may have additional ailments as you age and partly because the costs of medical procedures and medication increase over time. When doing costing on annual medical aid increases annually, use a rate of inflation plus 4% for these figures to be more accurate. Medical aid increases have historically been above the inflation rate, depending on the particular medical aid to which you belong, so cater to this cost wisely.

Action item 9: Stick to your strategy

Few people actively plan to create a bad ending but, as we've seen in this book, choosing not to plan is almost the same thing. If you're anything like me, you have made reminders to yourself of things you said you wanted to do but haven't got round to doing yet. We're really good at putting off things we know to be important when they don't feel particularly urgent. The sad truth is that things that don't seem to be too important often morph into something life-altering if they're ignored for too long. It is important to have a plan – and to be committed to seeing that plan come to pass. Be strategic in this life phase. The good news is that your financial planner will partner with you in creating and keeping you on track with your plan.

Action item 10: Be willing with your will

Wills and estate planning are to be taken seriously. For most of us, drawing up wills and thinking about estate planning are administrative headaches that we prefer to avoid. And yet, they are crucial to responsible financial planning. Most wills I come across are outdated or incorrectly drawn up, would you believe? I have met with clients who have proudly shown me their wills – only to discover, that in the 14 years they've had them, they have never been signed! The legal ramifications of poorly constructed – or unsigned – wills are not to be underestimated. A will that is not correctly witnessed on each page can be challenged to be invalid. We had such a case, and while the client was ultimately vindicated, it took time and legal fees to get to that resolution – completely unnecessary. So take the time out to ensure that your will is properly in order. Consider carefully who your executor should be: when you are no longer here, your choice as stated in your will cannot be changed by anyone, making it one of the most important decisions you will make.

I would strongly advise against a joint will. This is a will in which there is one will for both persons in the couple wherein they jointly reflect their wishes. A surviving spouse may have some difficulty in getting the original will from the Master's Office. And so we always suggest that both spouses should have separate wills, which mirror each other if they initially wanted to go the joint will route. The mirror wills will apply exactly the same provisos to each of the spouse's wills.

Here is how you know if your current will is valid:

- A will should be dated so that it can be ascertained which is the most recent will. In all subsequent wills, there should be a paragraph revoking all previous wills.
- A will must be signed by the testator (the person whose will it is) at the end – and on each page if there is more than one page.
- A will must be signed in the presence of at least two independent witnesses who are not mentioned in the will.
- Only the original will is valid – and it should therefore be stored in a safe place.
- Reviewing your will regularly is essential – especially in the case of any significant life changes such as marriage, divorce or the loss of a spouse. Check that your will still reflects your current wishes.
- If an amendment is added to the will at a later stage, the same requirements apply as with the original will in order to validate it.

Action item 11: Take trusts into account

Often clients do not own all their assets – they have set up trusts that own certain assets. A trust is a legal entity, brought to life by virtue of a trust instrument, through which control and ownership in property is made over or bequeathed to another person or persons (the trustees) for the benefit of the beneficiaries.

Make sure that your will speaks to your trust. It is crucial to take into account your trust deed when doing your retirement planning. Who are your current trustees? Who would be the replacement trustee should something happen? The answers to these questions should be integrated into your will. In addition, you should also consider what should be done with any loan accounts you may have with your trust. Previously, you could not leave these back to the trust without triggering capital gains tax, but legislation has now changed where you can leave a loan account back to the trust without this expense being incurred.

If trusts are not run properly, the estate planner runs the risk of SARS viewing the trust as a 'sham trust' and regarding all the assets as personal assets. Have regular trustee meetings that are minuted. Update the financials annually. A trust is a legal entity that is separate to you and your personal assets. So, having a separate financial plan for your trust in which the objectives of the trust are clear is helpful.

Action item 12: Enlighten yourself about Estate Duty

One of the questions I am asked is whether a person needs to pay Estate Duty or not. Estate Duty is a tax on the total market value of a person's assets (cash and non-cash) at the date of his or her death. Every person is entitled to the current legislated Estate Duty exemption on death, which means that Estate Duty only has to be paid if an estate is valued over a certain amount. If your estate is valued at more than this amount, Estate Duty is payable at 20%. Any assets that you leave to your spouse, even if they are in excess of the Estate Duty exemption, do not attract Estate Duty. Ask your planner what the exemption is at the time, as it changes.

If the first dying spouse leaves all his or her assets to the surviving spouse and doesn't use their Estate Duty exemption, when the second spouse dies, he or she will be entitled to use his or her own exemption, and the unused exemption of the previously deceased spouse. Estate Duty will then only be levied on amounts above the couples' combined exemptions. The value of your retirement funds (pension or provident funds, pension or provident preservation funds, retirement annuities and living annuities) does not form part of your dutiable estate, and is therefore not subject to estate duty.

If you wish to leave part of your estate to a PBO (Public Benefit Organisation), such as Guide Dogs or Animals in Distress, there is no estate duty payable as long as it is a qualifying PBO.

Action item 13: Deal with death

A useful question to ask yourself is: if I died last night, or my spouse did, how would my family be managing today? You need to have an in-case-of-death file. This is a file that your family opens should something untoward happen to you, something that can guide them through the necessary administration and logistics around what to do next.

Creating such a document – however difficult – is a practical way of helping ease some of the pain of your loved ones and allows them to mourn your death without the added financial stress related to funerals, accessing funds and making necessary payments. Winding up an estate can take months, so giving your loved ones easy access to necessary documents enables the process to be as efficient and manageable as possible. The folder, which should be kept somewhere safe and updated regularly or as you need to, should contain legal documents such as your will, organ donation information, your living will, financial documents, tax, bank account information, and personal documents like your ID. It should also contain your letter of wishes and any burial arrangements. Don't be afraid to encourage conversations on this topic with your family as part of your estate planning process as to what your will says and what your intentions are. As hard as it is for us to grasp, dying is as natural a process as birth and we don't need to be afraid of its implications.

Action item 14: Life happens – adapt!

Update your financial plan regularly. Life happens and, as transitions occur, make the necessary changes to keep your plan a living document.

The 14 Action Items for an A-Game Retirement are just the very basics of what needs to be taken into account when you design your financial plan. Exploring these steps would require two to three meetings with your financial planner, and may be the topic of my next book; certainly all these considerations would fill a whole book. These Action Items are a general indication of factors that need to be considered when writing a financial plan – I have made assumptions that may or may not apply to you. Please use these points to guide you and your planner as you customise your plan to match your needs.

What we have constructed together through this book is a plan of what you want your retirement to look like. Vitally important for this to work is for your money to be correctly invested and all of the 14 Action Items to be incorporated into your plan. However holistic your life plan may be, and however accurate your financial plan may be, they are worth so much more combined, resulting in retiremeant where money and meaning meet.

Concluding Thoughts

This book has been about exploring your life up to now and checking where it is going. And what a journey it has been. We have delved into much together, holding up the beliefs we cherish to the proverbial light of new perspectives and, as we have allowed ourselves to be open to the kaleidoscope of new colours and shapes that the world has to offer us, we have opened ourselves up along the way.

We have opened ourselves up to be more vulnerable and more soulful, more awestruck and more authentic. I trust that retirement looks a little different to you from when you first opened this book. I expect that it looks more meaningful; I long for you to see it as something to be anticipated and enjoyed, something to be explored and experienced.

And now it is over to you. Take each and every one of your most farfetched dreams and your financial specifics to a trustworthy planner and make your retirement a reality to you. I have loved being on this journey with you. Thank you for allowing me in.

Resources and Recommended Reading

I welcome you to make use of the Resources that we place at our clients' disposal. I have already mentioned the 18 Retiremeant Reflections that are available online. I encourage you to download them as you navigate your journey into retirement; here are other channels that will provide you with the same excellent updates and information to expand your knowledge ... and I am very happy to receive an email from you – in fact, I look forward to sharing your retirement journey.

Email me at: kim@retiremeant.co.za
Website address: www.retiremeant.co.za
Facebook: www.facebook.com/RetireSuccessfully

Please also visit our wesite www.retiresuccesfully.co.za. It has comprehensive lifestyle information from a team of retirementors on how to retire successfully. Here you can also subscribe to our monthly newsletter and weekly retirement tip.

I would love you to read more about the ideas I have written about in this book. They have revolutionised my view of retirement – in fact, of life – and I am sure you will find them equally informative, inspiring and, yes, challenging.

***Halftime* by Bob Buford, 2008, Zondervan**

Midlife. Halftime. It doesn't have to be a time of crisis. It can be a catalyst for purpose, impact, and growth. Bob Buford provides encouragement and insight to propel your life on a new course away from mere success to true significance – and the best years of your life.

***How Much is Enough? Money, Time, Happiness – a Practical Guide to Making the Right Choices* by Arun Abey, Andrew Bradley, and Andrew Ford, 2015**

How can millions of readers come to grips with their financial situation at a time when nothing seems to be enough? Arun Abey, Andrew Ford and Andrew Ford believe the answer lies beyond the balance sheet in the heart and spirit of the individual investor. Brilliantly combining economics and social thought, this book promises to revolutionise the investment world and gives readers the confidence to pursue their own paths toward a secure and fulfilling future.

***Making Life Matter – Living your dash!* by Dawie Smith, 2012, Naledi Books**

Themes addressed in this book include: an authentic and credible personal leadership model, understanding why you and other people think, feel and behave the way you and they do, learning to say "yes" to life and discovering your inborn talents and endowments.

***Teachings from the Apple Tree* by Colleen-Joy Page, 2005, Creda Communications**

In our modern world, worth is often measured by how much we have done things well enough. Like the apple tree, which fulfils its purpose by being all that it was born to be, we need to discover who we are. This book is a powerful and inspiring guide to finding meaning and living purposefully.

***The Couple's Retirement Puzzle: 10 Must-Have Conversations for Creating an Amazing New Life Together* by Roberta Taylor and Dorian Mintzer, 2014, Sourcebooks**
Roberta Taylor and Dorian Mintzer are relationship therapists and retirement coaches who have found that when couples are able to communicate effectively and know how to compromise and negotiate, they are less likely to avoid the often difficult and uncomfortable issues related to retirement transition.

***The 5 Love Languages* by Gary Chapman, 2010, Northfield Publishing**
New York Times bestselling author Dr Gary Chapman guides couples in identifying, understanding, and speaking their spouse's primary love language – quality time, words of affirmation, gifts, acts of service, or physical touch. By learning the five love languages, you and your spouse will discover your unique love languages and learn practical steps in truly loving each other.

***The New Retirementality* by Mitch Anthony, 2014, John Wiley & Sons**
Planning your life and living your dreams at any age you want. This is a book that redefines retirement and dispels all retirement myths.

The following three books have influenced my financial life-planning journey. I wholeheartedly recommend them to any financial planner looking to deepen his or her relationship with clients.

Financial Planning for Life: The Next Step: A Practical Approach to Merging Your Clients' Money with Their Lives **by Roy T Diliberto, 2006, FPA Press**

This book focuses on the way to structure a practice to ensure financial planners are concentrating on their clients' needs. A specialist in financial life planning, Diliberto challenges the notion of asset-centred financial planning in favour of the client-centred approach. He uses stories, personal examples, and wisdom from his career to discuss how to plan holistically, asking the questions: who is your client and what are their personal goals and needs? Not focused solely on the relationship with the client, Diliberto shines a bright light on the practice itself.

The Seven Stages of Money Maturity: Understanding the Spirit and Value of Money in Your Life **by George Kinder, 2000, Dell Publishing, Random House**

Discover a powerful way to look at your money and your life. Where do our attitudes to money come from, and how do they influence our lives? How can we approach financial issues with honesty and without fear?

Your Clients for Life **by Mitch Anthony, 2006, Dearborn Trade Publishing**

The financial services industry is changing as financial professionals face a growing demand to take a more client-centred approach. Clients are looking for more comprehensive guidance on how financial issues fit into a whole life plan. Seeking more than just return on investment, investors are proactively soliciting professional help in funding a lifestyle with satisfaction at its core.